The Baptism With The Holy Ghost

And I knew him not: but he that sent me to baptize with water, the same said unto me, Upon whom thou shalt see the Spirit descending, and remaining on him, the same is he which baptizeth with the Holy Ghost. -John 1:33

Ovit G. Pursley Ministries ®

Ovit G. Pursley, Sr.

The
Baptism
With The
Holy Ghost

Ovit G. Pursley, Sr.

Unless otherwise indicated, all Scripture quotations in this volume are from the *King James Version of* the Bible.

First Edition

First Printing 2010

Ovit G. Pursley Ministries®

11130 Kingston Pike, Suite 103

Knoxville, Tennessee 37934

Order this book online at www.trafford.com
or email orders@trafford.com

Most Trafford titles are also available at major online book retailers.

Printed in the United States of America.

ISBN: 978-1-4269-5560-0 (sc)
ISBN: 978-1-4269-5642-3 (e)

Trafford rev. 09/02/2011

 www.trafford.com

North America & International
toll-free: 1 888 232 4444 (USA & Canada)
phone: 250 383 6864 ♦ fax: 812 355 4082

CONTENTS

Chapter 1

What is the Baptism with the Holy Ghost?

Acts 1:5 For John truly baptized with water; but ye shall be baptized with the Holy Ghost not many days hence.

Acts 10:44-46 While Peter yet spake these words, the Holy Ghost fell on all them which heard the word. 45 And they of the circumcision which believed were astonished, as many as came with Peter, because that on the Gentiles also was poured out the gift of the Holy Ghost. 46 For they heard them speak with tongues, and magnify God.

Acts 11:15-17 And as I began to speak, the Holy Ghost fell on them, as on us at the beginning. 16 Then remembered I the word of the Lord, how that he said, John indeed baptized with water; but ye shall be baptized with the Holy Ghost. 17 Forasmuch then as God gave them the like gift as he did unto us, who believed on the Lord Jesus Christ; what was I, that I could withstand God?

Acts 19:2-6 He said unto them, Have ye received the Holy Ghost since ye believed? And they said unto him, We have not so much as heard whether there be any Holy Ghost. 3 And he said unto them, Unto what then were ye baptized? And they said, Unto John's baptism. 4 Then said Paul, John verily baptized with the baptism of repentance, saying unto the people, that they should believe on him which should come after him, that is, on Christ Jesus. 5 When they heard this, they were baptized in the name of the Lord Jesus. 6 And when Paul had laid his hands upon them, the Holy Ghost came on them; and they spake with tongues, and prophesied.

Hebrews 2:4 God also bearing them witness, both with signs and wonders, and with divers miracles, and gifts of the Holy Ghost, according to his own will?

Note: Caps and highlights are my emphasis.

1Corinthians 12:4, 11, 13 "Now there are diversities of gifts, but the same Spirit... But all these worketh that one and the selfsame Spirit, dividing to every man severally as he will... For by one Spirit are we all baptized into one body, whether we be Jews or Gentiles, whether we be bond or free; and have been all made to drink into one Spirit."

Luke 24:49 And, behold, I send the promise of my Father upon you: but tarry ye in the city of Jerusalem, until ye be endued with power from on high.

What is the Baptism with the Holy Ghost?
1. **The Promise of the Father.**
2. **The Promise of power.**
3. **Is the impartation of supernatural power and gifts for service?**
4. **The anointing of God upon the believer to work the works of Jesus Christ by the Word and Gifts of the Holy Spirit.**
5. **An operation of the Holy Spirit distinct from, addition to, and subsequent to His regenerating work.**

A number of phrases are used in the New Testament to describe one and the same experience:

1. "Baptized with the Holy Ghost."
2. "Filled with the Holy Ghost."
3. "The Holy Ghost fell on them."
4. "The gift of the Holy Ghost was poured out."
5. "Received the Holy Ghost."
6. "The Holy Ghost came on them."
7. "Gift of the Holy Ghost."
8. "I sent the promise of my Father unto you."
9. "Endued with power from on high."

Acts 19:2 He said unto them, Have ye Received the Holy Ghost since ye believed? And they said unto him, we have not so much heard whether there be any Holy Ghost.

The Baptism with the Holy Spirit is a definite experience.

One may and ought to know whether he or she has received the Baptism with the Holy Ghost or not. Many saints I question, have you receive the Baptism with the Holy Ghost? They respond; I have been baptized (referring to water baptism). They are ignorant about the teaching of being baptized with the Holy Ghost. It's not taught in their church. (No offence intended here.)

Compare to Acts 8:15-16— "Who, when they were come down, prayed for them, that they might receive the Holy Ghost: 16 (For as yet he was fallen upon none of them: only they were baptized in the name of the Lord Jesus.)" Galatians 3:2…"This only would I learn of you, Received ye the Spirit by the works of the law, or by the hearing of faith?"

Acts 1:5 For John truly baptized with water; but ye shall be baptized with the Holy Ghost not many days hence.

We see the same example of believers regenerated but not baptized with the Holy Ghost in Acts 19:1-2— "And it came to pass, that while Apollos was at Cotinth, Paul having passed through the upper coast, came to Ephesus; and finding certain disciples, 2 He said unto them, Have ye received the Holy Ghost since ye believed? And they said unto him, we have not so much as heard whether there be any Holy Ghost." Compare to verse 6— "And when Paul had laid his hands upon them, the Holy Ghost came on them; and they spake with tongues, and prophesied."

The Baptism with the Holy Ghost is an operation distinct from, additional to, and subsequent to His regenerating work.

One may be regenerated by the Holy Spirit and still not be baptized with the Holy Spirit. In regeneration there is an impartation of life (spiritual life), and the one who receives it is saved (born again); in baptism with the Holy Ghost there is an impartation of power to work the works of Christ by the Word and the Supernatural Gifts of the Holy Spirit. The one who receives it is anointed with the power and the anointing for service.

Every true believer has the Holy Spirit

Romans 8:9

But ye are not in the flesh, but in the Spirit, if so be that the Spirit of God dwell in you. Now if any man have not the Spirit of Christ, he is none of his.

1 Corinthians 6:9 What? Know ye not that your body is the temple of the Holy Ghost which is in you, which ye have of God, and ye are not your own?

But not every believer has the Baptism with the Holy Ghost, though every believer may. Not all believers receive the baptism with the Holy Ghost the same way. Note it is always according to the will of the Holy Spirit and not the way we minister to a person to receive.

The Baptism with the Holy Ghost may be received immediately during or after the new birth, (According to the will of the Holy Spirit) for example, in the house of Cornelius. Acts 10:44-46; "While Peter yet spake these words, the Holy Ghost fell on all them which heard the word. 45 And they of the circumcision which believed were astonished, as many as came with Peter, because that on the Gentiles also was poured out the gift of the Holy Ghost. 46 For they heard them speak with tongues, and magnify God."

In a normal state of the church, the baptism with the Holy Ghost would be received immediately upon repentance and baptism into the name of Jesus Christ for the remissions of sins (Acts 2:38). In many traditional churches the doctrine of the Baptism with the Holy Ghost has not been studied by the minister, or taught, and or the minister is claming we don't do that in our church. So, someone has to call the attention of the believers to their privilege in the risen Christ and claim it for them.

Acts 1:5, 8

For John truly baptized with water; but ye shall be baptized with the Holy Ghost not many days hence. But ye shall receive power, after that the Holy Ghost is come upon you: and ye shall be witnesses unto me both in Jerusalem, and in all Judaea, and in Samaria, and unto the uttermost part of the earth.

Luke 24:49 And, behold, I send the promise of my Father upon you: but tarry ye in the city of Jerusalem, until ye be endued with power from on high.

Acts 2:4 And they were all filled with the Holy Ghost, and began to speak with other tongues, as the Spirit gave them utterance.

Acts 9:17, 20

And Ananias went his way, and entered into the house; and putting his hands on him said, Brother Saul, the Lord, even Jesus, that appeared unto thee in the way as thou camest, hath sent me, that thou mightest receive thy sight, and be filled with the Holy Ghost. And straightway he preached Christ in the synagogues, that he is the Son of God.

1 Corinthians 12:4-14

Now there are diversities of gifts, but the same Spirit. 5 And there are differences of administrations, but the same Lord. 6 And there are diversities of operations, but it is the same God which worketh all in all. 7 But the manifestation of the Spirit is given to every man to profit withal. 8 For to one is given by the Spirit the word of wisdom; to another the word of knowledge by the same Spirit; 9 To another faith by the same Spirit; to another the gifts of healing by the same Spirit; 10 To another the working of miracles; to another prophecy; to another discerning of spirits; to another divers kinds of tongues; to another the interpretation of tongues: 11 But all these worketh that one and the selfsame Spirit, dividing to every man severally as he will. 12 For as the body is one, and hath many members, and all the members of that one body, being many, are one body: so also is Christ. 13 For by one Spirit are we all baptized into one body, whether we be Jews or Gentiles, whether we be bond or free; and have been all made to drink into one Spirit. 14 For the body is not one member, but many.

The baptism with the Holy Spirit is an experience connected with and primarily for the purpose of service.

The Baptism with the Holy Spirit has no direct reference to cleansing from sin. It has to do with gifts for service rather than with graces of character. (Even though there may be a healing or deliverance taking place during the Baptism with the Holy Ghost.)

Chapter 2

The Holy Ghost and Power

John 1:33

*33And I knew him not: but he that sent me to baptize with water, the same said **unto me,** Upon whom thou shalt set the Spirit descending, and remaining on him, the same is he which baptizeth with the Holy Ghost.*

Luke 3:16

16John answered, saying unto them all, I indeed baptize you with water; but one mightier than I cometh, the latcheth of whose shoes I am not worthy to unloose: he shall baptized you with the Holy Ghost and with fire:

Acts 2:38-39

*Then Peter **said unto them,** Repent, **and be baptized** even **one** of you in the name of Jesus Christ for the remission of sins, and ye shall receive the gift of the Holy Ghost. 39 For the promise is unto you, and to your children, and to all that are afar off, even as many as the Lord our God shall call.*

John 14:16-17

14If ye shall ask any thing in my name, I will do it. 15If you love me, keep my commandments. 16And I will pray the Father, and he shall give you another Comforter, that he may abide with you for ever; 1 7Even the Spirit of truth whom the world cannot receive, because it seeth him not neither knoweth him: but ye know him; for he dwelleth with you, and shall be in you.

The Baptism with the Holy Spirit is the "promise of the Father"(Acts 2: 38-39) in which Jesus promise to obtain when He ascended unto heaven. Jesus Himself, "commanded them that they should not depart from Jerusalem, but wait for the promise of the Father, which, saith he, ye have heard of me" (Acts 1:4). This promise was fulfilled on the day of Pentecost. "And they were all filled with the Holy Ghost, and began to speak with other tongues, as the Spirit gave them utterance" (Acts 2:4). This is the day the Holy Spirit came on His divine mission, a fulfillment of Joel 2:28, "And it shall come to pass afterward, that I will pour out my spirit upon all FLESH...."

The believer can be baptized with the Holy Spirit, and speak with other tongues as the Spirit gives utterance.

Jesus said, *"For John truly baptized with water; but ye shall be baptized with the Holy Ghost not many days hence"* (Acts 1:5). Again, this was fulfilled on the Day of Pentecost, *"And they were all filled with the Holy Ghost, and began to speak with other tongues, as the Spirit gave them utterance"* (Acts 2:4).

The Bible teaches that there are three baptisms available for every believer in the name of Jesus: (1) Baptism into the Body of Christ at the time of the new birth, (2) Baptism into water, (3) Baptism with the Holy Spirit. The latter is the one we will consider in this lesson.

I often point believers who have not studied the Bible very deeply, first, to Hebrews 5:11-14, then to Hebrews 6:1-3. In Hebrews chapter 6 we find the fundamental principles of the doctrine of Christ. One is called *"the doctrine of baptisms (v.2).*

Take just a minute and think back: God the Father had His ministry, He utilized the Prophets. God the Son used the Apostles and Disciples in His ministry. Now, the Holy Spirit has the Five-Fold Ministry (Ephesians 4:11). The Five-Fold Ministry *(Those who are called and anointed by God to stand in the Five-Fold Ministry Office) is* the primary ministry in the Body of Christ, *(therefore; every church should be a Five-Fold Ministry church)* in whom the Holy Spirit ministers through to the Body of Christ. Secondly, He ministers through those who are anointed with Spiritual Gifts (First Corinthians 12:4-11). Thirdly, the Holy Spirit ministers (bear witness) through those believers who become vessels of honor, by the Word of God and the Holy Spirit, meet for the Masters use.

Ephesians 4:11-15

"And he gave some, apostles; and some, prophets; and some, evangelists; and some, pastors and teachers; "For the perfecting of the saints, for the work of the ministry, for the edifying of the body of Christ: ¹³Till we all come in the unity of the faith, and of the knowledge of the Son of God, unto a perfect man, unto the measure of the stature of the fulness a Christ: "That we henceforth be no more children, tossed to and fro, and carried about with every wind of doctrine, by the sleight of men, and cunning craftiness, whereby they lie it wait to deceive."

1 Corinthians 12:4-11

"Now there are diversities of gifts, but the same Spirit. 'And there are differences of administrations, but the same Lord ⁶And there are diversities of operations, but it is the same God which worketh all in all. ⁷But the manifestation of the Spirit is given to every

man to profit withal. ⁸*For to one is given by the Spirit the word of wisdom; to another the word of knowledge by the same Spirit;* ⁹*To another faith by the same Spirit; to another the gifts of healing by the same Spirit* ¹⁰*To another the working of miracles; to another prophecy; to another discerning of spirits; to another divers kinds of tongues; to another the interpretation of tongues:* ¹¹*But all these worketh that one and the selfsame Spirit, dividing to every man severally as he will.*

We know that the Bible teaches that all born again Believers are baptized into the body of Christ. First Corinthian 12:13 says: *"For by one Spirit are we all baptized into and body, whether we be Jews or Gentiles, whether we be bond a free; and have been all made to drink into one Spirit.* Believes are also indwelled by the Holy Spirit at the time of the new birth. Also we know that the Holy Spirit, leads, guides, teaches, and keeps the believer.

So what is all this talk about the Baptism with the Holy Spirit? People are talking about it everywhere. Preachers and believers alike are asking; to whom was it given? Is it for us (the church) today? Can we prove it by the Bible? What did God say about it? What did John say about it? What did Jesus say about the Baptism with the Holy Ghost? What is the Baptism with the Holy Ghost for? How can I receive it? My question is would Jesus, Peter, John, and Paul say the same thing that you are saying about the Baptism with the Holy Ghost?

Key: Your duty as a born again believer is to say the same thing that God says according to His Word. You may not understand it, but it will give the Word and the Spirit free course to accomplish that He pleases. Hebrews 4:12 says: *"For the word of God is quick, and powerful, and sharper than any twoedged sword, piercing even to the dividing asunder of soul and spirit, and of the joints and marrow, and is a discerner of the thoughts and intents of the heart."* According to Hebrews 4:12, the power and ability of God is in His Word. Go with the Word of God, receive the Baptism with the Holy Ghost and become *a powerhouse* for God.

John 1:33

And I knew him not: but he that sent me to baptize with water, the same said unto me, **Upon whom thou shalt see the Spirit descending, and remaining on him, the same is he which baptizeth with the Holy Ghost.**

Acts 1:4-5

[4]*And, being assembled together with them, commanded them that they should not depart from Jerusalem, but* **wait for the promise of the Father,** *which, saith he, ye have heard of me. For John truly baptized with water; but* **ye shall be baptized with the Holy Ghost not many days hence.**

Acts 1:8

But ye shall receive power, after that the Holy Ghost is come upon you: *and ye shall be witnesses unto me both in Jerusalem, and in all Judaea, and in Samaria, and unto the* uttermost part of the earth.

Acts 2:38-39

Then Peter said unto them, Repent, and be baptized every one of you in the name of Jesus Christ for the remission of sins, **and ye shall receive the gift of the Holy Ghost.** [39] **For the promise is unto you, and to your children, and to all that are afar off, even as many as the Lord our God shall call**

John the Baptist was the first to speak prophetically, a message from the heart of God that believers would be *"baptized with the Holy Ghost."* This is one of the most significant phrases used in connection with the Holy Spirit in the scriptures. In speaking of himself and (Jesus) the coming One, he said:

I indeed baptize you with water unto repentance: but he that cometh after me is mightier than I, whose shoes I am not worthy to bear: **he shall baptize you with the Holy Ghost, and with fire.** Matthew 3:11

Some have question, if I receive the Baptism with the Holy Ghost should I expect to speak in tongues? If I speak in tongue should I speak a known language like they did on the day of Pentecost? Is there such a thing as unknown tongues? What is the primary difference in the tongue speaking on the day o Pentecost and that, which is spoken of in 1 Corinthians the 14" chapter?

My friend, tongue speaking (*other tongues* or *unknown tongues*) is the supernatural ability of the Holy Spirit given to some one to speak with other languages; (1.) *Other Tongues:* a known language that's unlearned by the speaker to minister to someone. (2.) *Unknown tongues* are primarily for your prayer life when you pray to God. Speaking in tongues by the Holy Spirit is always connected with the Baptism with the Holy Ghost. Speaking in tongue is the initial sign of receiving the Baptism with the Holy Ghost. As a matter of fact tongue speaking (the gift) and prophecy (the gift) are always associated with receiving the Baptism with the Holy Ghost.

I received the Baptism with the Holy Ghost and spoke in tongues when I was about (17) seventeen. Everyone that I have known to receive the Baptism with the Holy Ghost from that time on spoke in tongues. However, I do believe there and some who received the Baptism with the Holy Spirit that does not speak in tongues today. There are many reasons why. Some never develop their Gift. Others for the lack of use, still others have been taught that it is not for us to day. And I'm sure you could come up with a few reasons of your own.

Too many believers who are unlearned about tongue peaking are lead to believe that if you speak in tongues you must speak like they did on the Day of Pentecost (a known language). This is not true. Many also say that they do not believe in unknown tongues. The problem here is that they do not understand the difference in tongues on the Day of Pentecost and tongues in First Corinthians 14th chapter.

The answer to this dilemma is simple; on the Day of Pentecost, it was God by the power of the Holy Spirit ministering to the multitude through the 120 followers of Christ. In First Corinthians 14th chapter it is the believers (man) ministering *in the power of the Holy Spirit* to God.

First Corinthians 14:2 says; *"For he that speaketh in an unknown tongue speaketh not unto men, but unto God: for no man understandeth him; howbeit in the spirit he speaketh mysteries."*

Acts 2:4

And THEY were all filled with the Holy Ghost, and BEGAN TO SPEAK with other tongues, as the SPIRIT GAVE THEM UTTERANCE.

The Holy Spirit gives the utterance; you do the speaking. On the Day of Pentecost the Holy Spirit gave *them* the utterance; THEY (120 followers of Christ) did the speaking. "They" is the subject of Acts 2:4. *They* did the talking. The Holy Spirit gave *them* the utterance.

Acts 10:44-46

While Peter yet spake these words, the Holy Ghost fell on all them which heard the word. ⁴⁵And they of the circumcision which believed were astonished, as many as came with Peter, because that on the Gentiles also was poured out the gift of the Holy Ghost. ⁴⁶For **THEY HEARD THEM SPEAK WITH TONGUES,** and **Magnify** God.

Acts 19:6

⁶**And when Paul had laid** *his* **hands upon them, the Holy Ghost came on them; and THEY SPAKE WITH TONGUES, and prophesied.**

First, I challenge you and all believers to believe that the Baptism with the Holy Spirit that was poured out upon the 120 (Apostles and Disciples, both men and women) believers on the Day of Pentecost, to effectively proclaim Jesus Christ to the world, is still available to us today.

This *promise of the Father* was given to the whole church on the Day of Pentecost. If not, why do we see this *promise* falling upon Cornelius and his family, relatives and close friends, while Peter spoke the Word. Why is it that we see Peter and John ministering the Holy Spirit to the Samaritans? In Acts 19 why do we also see Apostle Paul doing the same thing with the Disciples of John the Baptist?

Acts 10:44

While Peter yet spake these words, the Holy Ghost fell on all them which heard the word. ⁴⁵*And they of the circumcision which* *believed were astonished, as many as came with Peter,* **because that on the Gentiles also was poured out the gift of the Holy Ghost.** [46]*For they heard them speak with tongues, and magnify God.* *Then answered Peter,* [47]*Can any man forbid water, that these should not be baptized,* **which have received the Holy Ghost as well as we?**

Acts 8:14-18

Now when the apostles which were at Jerusalem heard that Samaria had received the word of God, they sent unto them Peter and John: [15] **Who, when they were come down, prayed for them, that they might receive the Holy Ghost:** [16] **(For as yet he was fallen upon none of them: only they were baptized in the name of the Lord Jesus.)** [17] **Then laid they their hands on them, and they received the Holy Ghost.** [18] *And when Simon saw that through laying on of the apostles' hands the Holy Ghost was given, he offered them money,*

A careful study of the Old Testament reveals that the Holy Spirit was in operation at various times in the Old Testament, and that Prophets Work sign, wonders, and miracles. But the outpouring of the Holy Spirit as we know Him today was not manifest to the Old Testament Saints. Only three types of people in the Old Covenant had the Holy Spirit or the Anointing of God upon them: the King, Priest, and the Prophet. The followers of God or Old Testament Saints did not have the spirit of God.

On the other hand, we know from Bible teaching that the outpouring of the Holy Spirit is exclusive to the New Testament. John declared, *"One mighter than I cometh...He hall baptize you with the Holy Ghost and with fire"* (St. Luke 1:16). John also let us know that He (God) who sent him said, *"Upon whom thou shalt see the Spirit descending, and remaining on him, the same is he who baptizeth with the Holy Ghost* (St. John 1:33).

Later, Jesus said, *"But ye shall be baptized with the Holy Ghost not many days hence" (Acts 1:5)*. After Jesus had received of the Father the *promise of the Holy Ghost*, we find Peter proclaiming on the Day of Pentecost, *"He hath shed forth this (Holy Ghost) which ye now see and hear"* Acts 2:33).

Moreover, further study reveals that Peter let the multitude know on the Day of Pentecost that the same Spirit, the outpouring of the Holy Spirit **(The promise of the Father)** that they (the 120) received and possess are available unto every born again believer (Acts 2:38).

Notice closely what Peter says. *"For the promise is unto you, and your children, and to all that are afar off, even as many as the lord God shall call" (Acts 2:38)*.

Do not miss the point here. Acts 2:38 is only part of Peters message on the Day of Pentecost. Peter is talking about the, whole experience of the 120 (both men and women) in the upper room. As a matter of fact, Peter refers back o the Prophet Joel (Joel 2:28-29).

Peter is talking about more than just being born again. Peter is talking about being born again and baptized with the Holy Ghost for *"power."* Not every one that is born again and baptized into the body of Christ receives the Baptism with the Holy Ghost at the same time, to work the works of Christ. To become born again one must believe and receive Jesus Christ as their Lord and savior and repent of their sins. The Holy Spirit will then take up residence in them. This is called (being regenerated and born again) the New Birth.

There are many people who have believed and received Jesus Christ as Lord and Savior but have no *anointing* or *power* in his or her life. They have done all the right things according to the scripture. They believed, received, repented, confessed Jesus Christ as Lord and Savior, and have been baptized (water baptized). But, have no *power* or *anointing* in their lives. Why? Because this is called being born again: the New Birth.

The first qualification to receive the Baptism with the Holy Ghost, *the anointing of power for service is* to be born again. If you are born again then you are a prime candidate to receive the Baptism with the Holy Ghost. The Baptism with the Holy Ghost is received by faith just as the New Birth.

The scripture teaches us to *ask,* and *seek,* for what we desire from the Lord. Mark 11:24 says, *"Therefore I say unto you, What things soever ye desire, when ye pray, believe that ye receive them, and ye shall have them."* Knowing this, we can disregard all fears knowing that our Lord will not give us a counterfeit or substitute for the Holy Ghost.

Luke 11:11-13 [11]*If a son shall ask bread of any of you that is a father, will he give him a stone? or if he ask a fish, will he for a fish give him a serpent?* [12]*Or if he shall ask an egg, will he offer him a scorpion?* [13]*If ye then, being evil, know how to give good gifts unto your children: how much more shall your heavenly Father give the Holy Spirit to them that ask him?*

It is sad to say that many people are not in the knowledge that there is any Holy Ghost that they can receive today. Secondly, there are others who have been taught bad doctrine about the Baptism with the Holy Ghost. For example: They were taught such things as: (1) You received all the Holy Ghost that you need when you were born again. (2) You have to grow into that kind of power. (3) That was only for the apostles. (4) That died out with the Apostles. (5) We have the Bible now and there is no need for that now. (6) The Gifts and demonstration of power was just to get the church started. (7) There is no receiving of the Holy Ghost and speaking in tongues to day; that was for a sign on the day of Pentecost. I have even heard preachers and laymen alike say things like, well I have been in the church 15-20 years and I know that I'm saved. I don't need all that. I don't believe in it.

Have you heard these statements before? If your answer is yes, they are the teachings of men. First of all, the Bible does not teach any of those things just mention. I have heard them for years, but those statements; are not Bible based. *I challenge you to look up each one of those statements in the Bible to see if you can prove them to be the Word of God!* Secondly, Peter called receiving the Holy Ghost a "GIFT" (Acts 2:38). You can not grow into a gift: you receive it. Spiritual Gifts are given by the Holy Spirit according to the will of God. Thirdly, It is very clear in the scriptures that John the Baptist, Peter, Paul, and Jesus taught just the opposite concerning the Baptism with the Holy Ghost.

I beg of you not to add anything to the scripture or take anything away. Just believe and act on the Word of God and you will have the results of the Word. Acts 2:38 says, *"For the promise is unto you, and your children, and to all that are afar off,' even as many as the lord God shall call." (What promise is Peter referring to? Obviously: the Baptism with the Holy Ghost!)*

Your first step is to *believe* what the Bible says about it. Forget about what you believe and what you think, go with the WORD of GOD! Secondly, to receive the Baptism with the Holy Ghost just as John, Peter, Paul, and Jesus proclaimed it, (you must come into the knowledge that there is an experience following or subsequence to salvation called receiving, or Baptized with the Holy Ghost (see Acts 2:38; Acts 10:44-46).

Thirdly, you must also understand that it is the same Spirit that was in operation during the New Birth. However: a different manifestation for a different purpose. Let's put it this way that you may better understand it. First: the new birth (regeneration) for *salvation and life*. Secondly, the Baptism with the Holy Ghost or the anointing of the Holy Spirit for *Power, and service (Including worship, witnessing, preaching the word and teaching);* to work the works of Christ (*Including healing the sick, laying on of hands, deliverance, casting out devils*). What does God Want? He wants all of our ministry and service done in the power of the Holy Spirit.

Notice the manifestation of the Holy Spirit in First Corinthians 12:8-11. The Word of God let us know that it is the same Spirit, but a different manifestation, and different operation, each for a different purpose. When Jesus Baptize you with the Holy Ghost, it's a different operation of the Holy Spirit in regard to receiving the Holy Ghost at the time of the New Birth. Remember: one for *eternal life,* the other for the *endowment of power.* See Acts1:8.

Thousands upon Thousands who were born again have gone on to receive the Baptism with the Holy Ghost. They now have the anointing of God in their lives with a manifestation of the Ministry and Spiritual Gifts: with signs and miracles following (see Ephesians 4:11, 1 Corinthians 12:8-10). [It is sad to say that some Pastors do not understand when one in their congregation receives the Baptism with the Holy Ghost; I have heard them say, "O they thought they were saved, but they just got saved.] Another example is that I were in a church meeting one night, during the alter call, when several people came to the Alter to pray. I notice the young lady in front of me at the Alter in earnest praying seeking the Lord. The Spirit of the Lord was upon her. I told the Pastor, she is ready to receive (Referring to the Baptism with the Holy Ghost) He did not understand what I meant and thought that I was saying that she was called to preach.

To further open up our understanding of the Baptism with the Holy Ghost let us consider five scriptural witnesses. The Bible says, *"In the mouth of two or three witnesses every word may be established"* (Matthew 18:16).

In the next chapter let us note carefully what is being said, what is being done, and the results according to the following scriptures: (a) Acts 2:1-4); (b) Acts 8:14-18; (c) Acts 9:17); (d) Acts 10:44-46; (e) Acts 19:1-7.

Chapter 3

Baptized with the Holy Ghost

One of the primary purposes of this book is to show that the Scripture teaches two distinct operations of the Holy Spirit in regard to the New Birth and the Baptism with the Holy Ghost. The regeneration work of the Holy Spirit is for *salvation* and *eternal life:* The Baptism with the Holy Spirit for *power, and impartation of spiritual gifts* and *service.*

I want to list a few scriptures that show what *you* must do to be born again, that is, to obtain *salvation and life.* Then let us list a selection of scriptures that speaks about the Baptism with he Holy Ghost. This is important to see that there are two distinct operations of the Holy Spirit involved.

One operation for *salvation and life:* the other, for *power and service, and to impart Spiritual Gifts* to work the works of Christ. Beloved, after reading the next few scriptures you want find them saying anything about the Baptism with the Holy Ghost. Why, because these scriptures teach us about salvation and eternal life.

Salvation and life (New Birth-Born Again)

John 3:16

For God so loved the world, that he gave his only begotten Son, that whosoever believeth in him should not perish, but have everlasting life.

John 6:40

And this is the will of him that sent me, that every one which seeth the Son, and believeth on him, may have everlasting life: and I will raise him up at the last day.

John 5:24

Verily, verily, I say unto you, He that heareth my word, and believeth on him that sent me, hath everlasting life, and shall tot come into condemnation; but is passed from death unto life.

1 John 5:1

Whosoever believeth that Jesus is the Christ is born of God: and every one that loveth him that begat loveth him also that s begotten of him.

Mark 16:15-16

⁵And he said unto them, Go ye into all the world, and preach he gospel to every creature. ¹⁶He that believeth and is baptized shall be saved; but he that believeth not shall be damned.

Acts 16:30-31

°And brought them out, and said, Sirs, what must I do to be saved? ³¹And they said, Believe on the Lord Jesus Christ, and thou shalt be saved, and thy house.

Acts 4:12 Neither is there salvation in any other: for there is none other name under heaven given among men, whereby we must be saved.

John 3:3 Jesus answered and said unto him, Verily, verily, I say unto thee, Except a man be born again, he cannot see the kingdom of God.

John 3:4-7

Nicodemus saith unto him, How can a man be born when he is old? Can he enter the second time into his mother's womb, and be born? [5] Jesus answered, Verily, verily, I say unto thee, except a man be born of water and of the Spirit, he cannot enter into the kingdom of God. [6] That which is born of the flesh is flesh; and that which is born of the Spirit is spirit. Marvel not that I said unto thee, Ye must he born again.

Romans 1:16

For I am not ashamed of the gospel of Christ: for it is the power of God unto salvation to every one that believeth; to the Jew first, and also to the Greek.

Romans 10:9-10

That if thou shalt confess with thy mouth the Lord Jesus, and shalt believe in thine heart that God hath raised him from the dead, thou shalt be saved. [10] For with the heart man believeth unto righteousness; and with the mouth confession is made unto salvation.

Romans 10:13

For whosoever shall call upon the name of the Lord shall be saved.

Titus 2:11

For the grace of God that bringeth salvation bath appeared to all men.

Hebrews 1:14

Are they not all ministering spirits, sent forth to minister for them who shall be heirs of salvation?

2 Corinthians 5:17

Therefore if any man *be* in Christ, *he is* a new creature: old things are passed away; behold, all things are become new.

2 Corinthians 5:21

For he hath made him *to be* sin for us, who knew no sin; that we might be made the righteousness of God in him.

Ephesians 2:1

And you *hath he quickened,* who were dead in trespasses and sins.

1 Timothy 2:3-4

For this is good and acceptable in the sight of God our Saviour; who will have all men to be saved, and to come unto the knowledge of the, truth.

1 John 2:1-2

My little children, these things write I unto you, that ye sin not. And if any man sin, we have an advocate with the Father, Jesus Christ the righteous: 2 And he is the propitiation for our sins: and not for our only, but also for *the sins of* the whole world.

Colossians 2:13
And you, being dead in your sins and the uncircumcision of your fleshhath he quickened together with him, having forgiven you all trespasses.

The scriptures just mention is overwhelming clear about what the Bible teaches about *salvation and life.* In most salvation scriptures you will find words like, "believe," "believeth," "confess," "repent," "be baptized," call on the name of Jesus, "and according to Acts 16:31; *"Believe on the Lord Jesus Christ, and thou shalt be saved and thy house."*

My friend: that's what it takes to be saved! These scriptures teach us what *you* must do in order to have salvation, eternal life, everlasting life, born again, and the new birth. Did you notice that these scriptures did not say anything about being *baptized with the Holy Ghost?* Why, because they are talking about the regeneration work of the Holy Spirit.

What Happens when we are Saved, Born again, or Receive Jesus as our personal Lord and Savoir?

Once we truly believe in our heart, and confess with our mouth the Lord Jesus, the Holy Ghost began to move on our behalf. The Holy Ghost reaches over into the Kingdom of Darkness (Satan Kingdom), and translates us out of the Kingdom of Darkness, (because Satan no longer has a legal hold on us, as our god) and emerges (baptize) us into the Kingdom of His dear Son. Thus, we are born again -saved.

Who hath delivered us from the power of darkness, and hath translated us into the kingdom of his dear Son. –*Colossians 1:13.* **This now begins our new life in Jesus Christ.**

John 14:16-17
And I will pray the Father, and he shall give you another Comforter that he may abide with you for ever; 17 Even the Spirit of truth; whom the world cannot receive, because it seeth him not, neither knoweth him: but ye know him; for he dwelleth with you, and shall be in you.

Things That Happen at Conversion
Key: At this point you must fully understand what take place at the time of your conversion; when you are born again, or receive eternal life (John 3:16; John 6:40; John 5:24).

In an instant, the life of a person is transformed through a personal relationship with Jesus Christ.

Now, let us compare what the scripture says about salvation with that of the Baptism with the Holy Ghost.

Baptism with the Holy Ghost (Power-authority for Service, and impartation of spiritual gifts.
See Acts 1:8)

Mat 3:11

I indeed baptize you with water unto repentance: but he that cometh after me is mightier than I, whose shoes I am not worthy to bear: he shall baptize you with the Holy Ghost, and with fire:

John 1:33

And I knew him not. but he that sent me to baptize with water, the same said unto me, Upon whom thou shalt see the Spirit descending, and remaining on him, the same is he which baptizeth with the Holy Ghost.

Acts 1:5

For John truly baptized with water; but ye shall be baptized with the Holy Ghost not many days hence.

Acts 1:8

But ye shall receive power, after that the Holy Ghost is come upon you. and ye shall be witnesses unto me both in Jerusalem, and in all Judaea, and in Samaria, and unto the uttermost part of the ea'th.

Acts 2:32-33

This Jesus hath God raised up, whereof we all are witnesses. [32] Therefore being by the right hand of God exalted, and having received of the Father the promise of the Holy Ghost, he hath shed forth this, which ye now see and hear.

Acts 2:38

Then Peter said unto them, Repent, and be baptized every one of you in the name of Jesus Christ for the remission of sins, and ye shall receive the gift of the Holy Ghost.

He shall baptize you with the Holy Ghost

Luke 3:16

John answered, saying unto them all, I indeed baptize you with water, but one mightier than I cometh, the latchet of whose shoes I am not worthy to unloose: he shall baptize you with the *Holy Ghost and with fire:*

John declared who will baptize with the Holy Ghost

John 1:33

And I knew him not: but he that sent me to baptize with water, he same said unto me, Upon whom thou shalt see the Spirit descending, and remaining on him, the same is he which baptizeth with the Holy Ghost.

Jesus promise the Holy Ghost and Power

Notice that in this text it mentions receiving power to witness v8.

Acts 1:5, 8

For John truly baptized with water; but ye shall be baptized with the Holy Ghost not many days hence....But ye shall receive power, after that the Holy Ghost is come upon you: and ye shall be witnesses unto me both in Jerusalem, and in all Judaea, and in Samaria, and unto the uttermost part of the earth.

Jesus acquire the Holy Ghost

Acts 2:32-33

This Jesus hath God raised up, whereof we all are witnesses. **33** therefore being by the right hand of God exalted, and having received of the Father the promise of the Holy Ghost, he hath shed forth this, which ye now see and hear.

The Holy Ghost promise to all believers

Acts 2:38-39

Then Peter said unto them, Repent, and be baptized every one of you in the name of Jesus Christ for the remission of sins, and ye shall receive the gift of the Holy Ghost. [39] For the promise is unto you, and today to your children, and to all that are afar off even as many as the Lord our God shall call.

Again, we notice that the scriptures just mention has very little to say about being born again, or eternal life. You will have to agree that these scriptures are talking about the *"Promise of the Father,* "the Baptism with the Holy Ghost for POWER and SERVICE. (Acts 1:8) Power for service: to work the works of Christ. You cannot have miracles, signs, wonders, healing, and deliverance following your ministry without the **"Anointing POWER."** **of the "Holy Ghost."**

Now, I will list five scriptures that we will consider in the next chapter. These scriptures can change your life. This is where the "POWER" come in. *"But ye shall receive power, after that the Holy Ghost is come upon you"* (Acts 1:8).

On The Day of Pentecost
Acts 2:1-4

And when the day of Pentecost was fully come, they were all with one accord in one place. 2 And suddenly there came a sound from heaven as of a rushing mighty wind, and it filled all the house where they were sitting. 3 And there appeared unto them cloven tongues like as of fire, and it sat upon each of them. 4 And they were all filled with the Holy Ghost, and began to speak with other tongues, as the Spirit gave them utterance.

Philip, Peter, and John at Samaria
Acts 8:14-18

Now when the apostles which were at Jerusalem heard that Samaria had received the word of God, they sent unto them Peter and John: 15 Who, when they were come down, prayed for them, that they might receive the Holy Ghost: 16 (For as yet he was fallen upon none of them: only they were baptized in the name of the Lord Jesus.) 17 Then laid they their hands on them, and they received the Holy Ghost. 18 And when Simon saw that through laying on of the apostles' hands the Holy Ghost was given, he offered them money,

Ananias with Paul at Damascus
Acts 9:17

And Ananias went his way, and entered into the house; and putting his hands on him said, Brother Saul, the Lord, even Jesus, that appeared unto thee in the way as thou camest, hath sent me, that thou mightest receive thy sight, and be filled with the Holy Ghost.

Peter at Cornelius House

Acts 10:44-47

While Peter yet spake these words, the Holy Ghost fell on all them which heard the word. [45] *And they of the circumcision which believed were astonished, as many as came with Peter, because that on the Gentiles also was poured out the gift of the Holy Ghost.* [46] *For they heard them speak with tongues, and magna God. Then answered Peter,* [47] *Can any man forbid water, that these should not be baptized, which have received the Holy Ghost as well as we?*

Paul at Ephesus

Acts 19:1-7

And it came to pass, that, while Apollos was at Corinth, Paul having passed through the upper coasts came to Ephesus: and finding certain disciples, [2] *He said unto them, Have ye received the Holy Ghost since ye believed? And they said unto him, we have not so much as heard whether there be any Holy Ghost. And he said unto them, Unto what then were ye baptized? And they said, Unto John's baptism.* [4] *Then said Paul, John verily baptized with the baptism of repentance, saying unto the people, that they should believe on him which should come after him, that is, on Christ Jesus.* [5] *When they heard this, they were baptized in the name of the Lord Jesus.* [6] *And when Paul had laid his hands upon them, the Holy Ghost came on them; and they spake with tongues, and prophesied. 7 And all the men were about twelve.*

Keep reading, in the next chapter we will pick these scriptures apart that we may obtain the truth about what was said, what was done, and the results.

Chapter 4

The Promise of Power

On The Day of Pentecost

And when the day of Pentecost was fully come, they were all with one accord in one place. [2] *And suddenly there came a sound from heaven as of a rushing mighty wind, and it filled al the house where they were sitting.* [3] *And there appeared unto them cloven tongues like as of fire, and it sat upon each o them.* [4] *And they were all filled with the Holy Ghost, and begat to speak with other tongues, as the Spirit gave them utterance* (Acts 2:1-4).

Acts 2:1-4

(A) What were the Apostles and the others doing when the Day of Pentecost was fully come: when the Holy Spirit came?

Answer: (v.1) *"They were all with one accord in one place."*

(B) What happen at this time?

Answer: (v.2) *"And suddenly there came a sound from heaven as a rushing mighty wind, and it filled all the house when they were sitting."*

(C) What happen next?

Answer: (v.3) *"And there appeared unto them cloven of tongues like as of fire, and it sat upon each of them."*

There is an important word in the answer of the text (v.3) that word is *cloven*. It is rendered split or parted. See also the word *cleave*. The Greek word is Kleben. Taking another look at the word cloven, it is rendered: split or divided.

It is evident then that those receiving the Holy Ghost received various tongues or languages (that they did not normally speak) and they spoke them as the Holy Spirit gave them utterance.

(D) What were the 120 people in the upper room filled with?

Answer: (v.4) *"They were all filled with the Holy Ghost"*

(E) After being filled with the Holy Ghost what did they do?

Answer: (v.4) *"They began to speak with other tongues."*

(F) How were they able to speak in other tongues or languages?

Answer: (v.4) *"As the Spirit gave them utterance."*

Key: When they were filled, they began to speak with other tongues as the Spirit gave them utterance. Notice; first come the anointing, power, filling, then, the ability to perform.

NOTE: *No one can teach you how to speak in tongues.* It's a work or manifestation of the Holy Spirit. **Any thing else is a counterfeit.**

Philip manifest the Power of God in Samaria

Acts 8:5-8

Then Philip went down to the city of Samaria, and preached Christ unto them. ⁶ And the people with one accord gave heed unto those things which Philip spake, hearing and seeing the miracles which he did. For unclean spirits, crying with loud voice, came out of many that were possessed with them. And many taken with palsies, and that were lame, were healed. 8 And there was great joy in that city. (Note: First the ANOINTING and the POWER: then the ability to perform).

(A) What happen when Philip preached Christ in Samaria?

Answer: (v.6) *"The people with one accord gave heed unto those things which Philip spake, hearing and seeing the miracles which he did".*

(B) What miracles did Philip perform in the power of the Spirit?

Answer: (v.7) *"Unclean spirits, crying with loud voice, came out of many that were possesed with them: and taken with palsies, and that were lame, were healed".*

Philip Preach the Kingdom of God and the Name of Jesus Christ in Samaria

Acts 8:9-13

But there was a certain man, called Simon, which beforetime in the same city used sorcery, and bewitched the people of Samaria, giving out that himself was some great one: [10] *To whom they all gave heed, from the least to the greatest, saying This man is the great power of God.* [11] *And to him they had regard, because that of long time he had bewitched them with sorceries.* [12] *But when they believed Philip preaching the things concerning the kingdom of God, and the name of Jesus Christ, they were baptized, both men and women.* [13] *Then Simon himself believed also: and when he was baptized, he continued with Philip, and wondered, beholding the miracle: and signs which were done.*

(A) What happen when the Samaritans believed Philip'; preaching the things concerning the Kingdom of God, and the name of Jesus Christ?

Answer: (v.12) *"They were baptized, both men and women."*

(B) What happen when Simon saw the miracles and heard Philip preach the things concerning the Kingdom of God and the Name of Jesus Christ?

Answer: (v.13) *"Then Simon himself believe also: and when he was baptized, he continued with Philip, and wonders beholding the miracles and signs which were done ".*

The Apostles sent Peter and John to Samaria
Acts 8:14-18

Now when the apostles which were at Jerusalem heard that Samaria had received the word of God, they sent unto then *Peter and John: 'Who, when they were come down, prayed for them, that they might receive the Holy Ghost:* [16] *(For as yet he was fallen upon none of them: only they were baptized in the name of the Lord Jesus.)* [1] *Then laid they their hands on them, and they received the Holy Ghost.* ¹⁸ *And when Simon saw that through laying on of the apostles' hands the Holy Ghost was given, he offered them money,*

(A) What happen when the Apostles at Jerusalem heard that Samaria had received the word of God?

Answer: (v.14) *"They sent Peter and John unto them."*

(B) What did Peter and John do when they arrived in Samaria?

Answer: (v.15) *"Who, when they were come down, prayed for them that they might receive the Holy Ghost."*

Key: The Samaritans had heard the word (faith comes by hearing). They believed and was baptized (Mark 16:16), and the Spirit of Christ took up resident in them. They were delivered from the Kingdom of Darkness and translated unto the Kingdom of His dear Son. (Col. 1:13)

These Samaritans were born again baptized believers, both men and women (v.12). Jesus said. *"Go ye into all the world, and preach the gospel to every creature. He that believeth and is baptized shall be saved; but he that believeth not shall be damned"* (Mark 16:15-16). These Samaritans had believed and were baptized. According to the words of Jesus they were already saved when Peter and John arrived. This is the point you can't get people to see. They were already saved when Peter and John came down from Jerusalem. It is obvious that something else happen beside the New Birth.

The answer is so simple that people stumble all over it. **For example: we never lay hands on anyone to be born again, or for them to receive the regeneration work of the Holy Spirit after making confession of Jesus Christ.** *But, for the most part, we always lay hands on people to impart the Holy Spirit to bless them, for power, healing, and deliverance, but never for them to be saved.* The scripture teaches us that, *"For by grace are ye saved through faith; and that not of yourselves: it is the gift of God."* (Ephesians 2:8). If you are still not convinced that something took place beside the new birth; then consider Simon, he saw that it was more to it than just believing on Jesus. What he saw was the demonstration of the power of God!

(C) After praying for them, what else did Peter and John do?

Answer: (v.7) *"Then laid their hands on them, and they receive the Holy Ghost."*

Note: This is a group of believers receiving the baptism with the Holy Ghost after being saved by the laying on of hands by Peter and John.

It is worthy to note here that the putting on of hands (to impart the Holy Spirit) is one way a believer may receive the Holy Ghost. However, some church groups may use various methods in helping believers receive the Baptism of the Holy Ghost; nevertheless, there is no set pattern. One believer may receive differently from another even in the same place at the same time. Remember, even though one may be instrumental in helping a believer receive the Holy Ghost, it is always according to the will of the Spirit and not according to the way we minister unto them.

Let us consider another aspect of laying on of hands. Notice in Hebrews 6:2, one of the primary doctrines of Jesus Christ is the *doctrine of laying on of hands*. As a matter of fact the laying on of hands is a doctrine from the Old Testament to the New Testament. But, for our lesson sake, let us consider the New Testament examples.

In the New Testament we see that laying on of hands was used in five ways: (1) in connection with miracles of healing (28:8; Matt. 9:18; Mark 5:23, 6:5): (2) in blessing others (Matt. 19:13,15); (3) in connection with the baptism with the Holy Ghost (Acts 18:17,19; 19:6); in commissioning for a specific work (Acts 6:6; 13:3); and (5) in imparting spiritual gifts by the Elders (1 Tim. 4:14). Beloved saints, we can see that the laying on of hands is one of many means by which God mediates gifts and blessings to others. Laying on of hands (a doctrine of Jesus Christ, Hebrews 6:2) became a foundation doctrine in the early church. Note: Lay hands on no man with out the unction of the Holy Spirit.

Note: If you do not believe in or practice laying on of hands in your church, then you are failing to exercise a foundation doctrine of Jesus Christ (Hebrews 6:1-3).

It doesn't matter what your denomination is. Man should obey God (The Holy Scriptures in the work of the church) rather than man. Get and oil bottle, Lay hands on it and pray over it to consecrate it. Then anoint the sick with oil (according to the scripture), then lay your hands on them in the power of the Spirit believing, and command the sickness to depart from them in the name of JESUS. But remember Jesus is the healer, not you. If he heals when you ask Him to do so, we bless Him the more. If he doesn't heal at that moment we know that He can. If you practice this in the name of Jesus you will see a greater work of the Holy Spirit in you church or ministry.

Chapter 5

Conversion, Commission, and Power

Saul of Tarsus on Damascus Road

In Acts chapter nine we find the story of Saul of Tarsus who had an encounter with the Lord Jesus Christ on the Damascus road. Subsequently, the Lord said unto him, *"arise, and go into the city, and it shall be told thee what thou must do"* (Acts 9:6),

Acts 9:1-9

And Saul, yet breathing out threatenings and slaughter against, the disciples of the Lord, went unto the high priest, And desired of him letters to Damascus to the synagogues, that if he found any of this way, whether they were men or women, he might bring them bound unto Jerusalem. And as he journeyed, he came near Damascus: and suddenly there shined round about him a light from heaven: And he fell to the earth, and heard a voice saying unto him, Saul, Saul, why persecutes thou me? `5` *And he said, Who art thou, Lord? And the Lord said I am Jesus whom thou persecutest: it is hard for thee to kick against the pricks.* `6` *And he trembling and astonished said, Lord, what wilt thou have me to do? And the Lord said unto him, Arise, and go into the city, and it shall be told them what thou must do. And the men which journeyed with him stood speechless, hearing a voice, but seeing no man.* `8` *And Saul arose from the earth; and when his eyes were opened, he saw no man: but they led him by the hand,*

and brought him into Damascus. ⁹ *And he was three days without sight, ant neither did eat nor drink.*

(A) What was Saul of Tarsus on his way to do in Damascus?

Answer: (v2) "And desired of him letters to Damascus to the synagogues, that if he found any of this way, whether they were men or women, he might bring them bound unto Jerusalem."

(B) When Saul encountered the Lord on Damascus road, what did the Lord say to him?

Answer: (v4-7) "And he fell to the earth, and heard a voice saying unto him, Saul, Saul, why persecutest thou me? ⁵ And he said, Who art thou, Lord? And the Lord said, I am Jesus whom thou persecutest: it is hard for thee to kick against the pricks. And he trembling and astonished said, Lord, what wilt thou have me to do? And the Lord said unto him, Arise, and go into the city, and it shall be told thee what thou must do. And the men which journeyed with him stood speechless, hearing a voice, but seeing no man."

The Lord commission Ananias
Acts 9:10-12

And there was a certain disciple at Damascus, named Ananias; and to him said the Lord in a vision, Ananias. And he said, Behold, I am here, Lord. ¹¹ And the Lord said unto him, Arise, and go into the street which is called Straight, and inquire in the house of Judas for one called Saul, of Tarsus: for, behold, he prayeth, ¹² And hath seen in a vision a man named Ananias coming in, and putting his hand on him, that he might receive his sight.

Acts 9:17-20

And Ananias went his way, and entered into the house; and putting his hands on him said, Brother Saul, the Lord, even Jesus, that appeared unto thee in the way as thou camest, hath sent me, that thou mightest receive thy sight, and he filled with the Holy Ghost. [18]And immediately there fell from his eyes as it had been scales: and he received sight forthwith, and arose, and was baptized. And when he had received meat, he was strengthened. Then was Saul certain days with the disciples which were at Damascus. [20]And straightway he preached Christ in the synagogues, that he is the Son of God.

(A) Upon receiving instructions from the Lord in a vision, what did Ananias do?

Answer: (v.17) *"And Ananias went his way, and entered into the house; and; putting his hands on him said, Brother Saul the Lord, even Jesus, that appeared unto the in the way as thou camest, hath sent me, that thou mightest receive thy sight, and be filled with the Holy Ghost. "*

(B) What may we conclude by reading Acts 9:17-20?

Answer: We may conclude that:

(1) Saul believed Ananias report.

(2) Immediately received his sight.

(3) Arose-got up from the praying position.

(4) Were born again.

(5) Were baptized.

(6) Filled with the Holy Ghost.

(7) Broke his fast-at food to regain his strength.

(8) Continued certain days with the Disciples at Damascus.

(9) And straightway he preached Christ in the synagogues; that he is the Son of God.

Peter Preaches at Cornelius House

Acts 10:44-46

While Peter yet spake these words, the Holy Ghost fell on all them which heard the word. [45] *And they of the circumcision which believed were astonished, as many as came with Peter because that on the Gentiles also was poured out the gift of the, Holy Ghost.* [46] *For they heard them speak with tongues, am magnified God.*

(A) What happen while Peter was preaching to Cornelius an his house, kindred, and friends?

Answer: (v.44) *"While Peter yet spake these words, the Holy Ghost fell on all them which heard the word."*

(B) Those who came with Peter of the circumcision that believed were astonished, why?

Answer: (v.45) *"Because that on the gentiles also was poured out the gift of the Holy Ghost, for they heard them speak with tongues, and magnify God"*

(C) What convinced those of the circumcision that the Gentiles had received the Holy Ghost?

Answer: (v.45) *"They heard then speak with tongues, and magnify God"*

Note: This is a case where another group of believers received the baptism with the Holy Ghost at the same time (Jerusalem/Cornelius House).

Paul found certain Disciples at Ephesus

Acts 9:1-7

And it came to pass, that, while Apollos was at Corinth, Paul laving passed through the upper coasts came to Ephesus: and finding certain disciples, He said unto them, Have ye received the Holy Ghost since ye believed? And they said unto him, We have not so much as heard whether there be any Holy ghost. [3] And he said unto them, Unto what then were ye baptized? And they said, Unto John's baptism. [4] Then said Paul, John verily baptized with the baptism of repentance, saying unto the people, that they should believe on him which should come after him, that is, on Christ Jesus. [5] When they heard this, they were baptized in the name of the Lord Jesus. [6] And when Paul had laid his hands upon them, the Holy Ghost came on them; and they spake with tongues, and prophesied [7] And all the men were about twelve.

A) When Paul found twelve disciples of John in Ephesus, what did he ask them?

Answer: (v.2) "He said unto them, have you received the Holy Ghost since ye believed?"

B) What was their reply?

Answer: (v.2) *"We have not so much as heard whether there be any Holy Ghost."*

C) Paul said unto them, unto what then was ye baptized?

Note: Paul's question here is directed toward water baptism.

Answer: (v.3) *"And they said, unto Johns baptism."*

Note: John's baptism - emerged in water: a baptism of repentance for the remission of sins.

(D) When the disciples at Ephesus heard Paul's teaching concerning John's baptism, and that they should believe on Christ Jesus, what did they do?

Answer: (v.5) *"They were baptized in the name of the Lord Jesus."*

Note: Water Baptism (the Christian baptism) (see Mark 16:16, Matthew 28:19). Note also that after Paul baptized them in the name of Jesus, "the Christian baptism" he was free to lay his hands on them to impart the Baptism with the Holy Ghost.

(E) What did Paul do immediately after they were baptized in the name of the Lord Jesus?

Answer: (v.6) "Paul laid his hands upon them."

(F) Why did Paul lay his hands upon them?

Answer: (v.6) "He laid his hands upon them that they might receive the Holy Ghost."

(G) What happen when he laid his hands upon them?

Answer: (v.6) *"The Holy Ghost came on them."*

(H) What took place immediately after the disciples at Ephesus received the Holy Ghost?

Answer: (v.6) "They spake with tongues and prophesied, and all the men were about twelve."

I thank the Holy Spirit for His leading in the questions and answers in each session. Every answer is directly by the scriptures. No guessing game here! To some, it might seem that the questions here are insignificant. But, I am trying to make a point.

It is important to note what Paul did. For example: (1) Paul question them about the Holy Spirit. He knew that they were disciples. (2) He questions them about their baptism to gain more knowledge, and to find a good starting point to open up their understanding. (3) Paul then started with the baptism of John and ended up with Jesus Christ. (4) The disciples were told to believe on the Lord Jesus. Paul reminded them that John taught that there would be one coming after him. (5) They believed and confessed. Paul then baptized them (John 3:15-16; John 3:18; John 3:36; John 6:47; Matthew 28:19) in the name of the Lord Jesus (the Christian baptism for remissions of sins). (6) After their baptism, Paul laid his hands upon them to impart the Holy Spirit for "Power". Not to be "Born Again" (Mark 16:16), but for "Power" (Acts 1:8).

The twelve disciples of John had the same experience of the Baptism with the Holy Ghost, as did the others before them. They were not only "Born Again," they received "Power." For example: It took the power of the Holy Spirit for them to supernaturally speak in tongues and to prophesy (Acts 19:6-7). Remember; first come the saving; then the anointing; in other words the power.

Note: Hear again, we see a group of believers receiving the baptism with the Holy Ghost by the hands of Paul.

Now, let us examine the Word of God. Take a close look at the scriptural phrases used in each text we considered. I believe according to the truth, the "WORD" of God, the terms used in the five scripture phrases all refer to the same experience; *"the promise of the Father,"* the Baptism with the Holy Ghost. Let's take another look at the word.

Notice the following scriptural phrases: (caps, my emphasis)

(A) **On the Day of Pentecost:** Acts 2:4 "And they were all FILLED with the Holy Ghost."

(B) **Philip, Peter and John at Samaria:** Acts 8:17 "And they RECEIVED the Holy Ghost."

(C) **Ananias with Paul at Damascus:** Acts 9:17 "And Be FILLED with the Holy Ghost."

(D) **Peter at Cornelius House:** Acts 10:44 "The Holy Ghost FELL on all them which heard the word."

(E) **Paul in Ephesus:** Acts 19:1-7 "The Holy Ghost CAME on them."

Some say that you don't find any one receiving the Baptism with the Holy Ghost after Acts 19 in the Bible. The reason being is that by the time of Paul's ministry; receiving the Baptism with the Holy Ghost was the norm. If the Holy Ghost didn't fall upon one at the time of the new birth someone ministered it unto them shortly there after.

Truly, this lesson is a blessing from God. Thanks, be to God, and our Lord and Savior Jesus Christ, and the Holy Spirit. We should know now what the WORD of God has to say about the Baptism with the Holy Ghost.

Chapter 6

How to receive the Baptism With the Holy Ghost

My friend, if you have studied this book to this point and have not already received the Baptism with the Holy Ghost, now is the time! Simply believe the Word of God, and then ask in faith the Lord Jesus to baptize you with the Holy Ghost. (See Acts 2:32-33)

John 14:16, 17

And I will pray the Father, and he shall give you another Comforter that he may abide with you for ever; 17 Even the Spirit of truth; whom the world cannot receive, because it seeth him not, neither knoweth him: but ye know him; for he dwelleth with you, and shall be in you.

Acts 2:1, 4

And when the day of Pentecost was fully come, they were all with one accord in one place. And suddenly there came a sound from heaven as of a rushing mighty wind, and it filled all the house where they were sitting. ³And there appeared unto them cloven tongues like as of fire, and it sat upon each of them. ⁴And they were all filled with the Holy Ghost, and began to speak with other tongues, as the Spirit gave them utterance.

Acts 2:32, 33

²This Jesus hath God raised up, whereof we all are witnesses. *³³Therefore being by the right hand of God exalted, and having received of the Father the promise of the Holy Ghost, he hath shed forth this, which ye now see and hear.*

We have already learned from the word of God; and John the Baptist about this Baptism with the Holy Ghost (John 1:33; Luke 3:16; Matthew 3:11). Secondly, we have the witness of Jesus. Jesus said His followers would be baptized with the Holy Ghost (Acts 1:4-5; Acts 1:8; John 14:16-17; Luke 11:11-3). Thirdly, we have the witness of Peter (Acts 2:38-39; Acts 10:44-46; Acts 8:14-18). Fourthly, we have the witness of Paul Acts 19:1-7).

The Holy Spirit came on His divine mission on the Day of Pentecost. Thus, fulfilling the WORD'S of Jesus: *"For John truly with water; but ye shall be baptized with the Holy Ghost not many days hence."*

We do not have to pray the Holy Spirit down from heaven or ask the Lord to send Him down. The Holy Spirit is already in the world and indwells every born again believer.

What we are looking for is the anointing of POWER! If you want the power of God for *service and to work the works of Jesus Christ,* then you need to receive the Baptism with the Holy Ghost. You cannot have signs, miracles, healing, and deliverance following your ministry without the anointing of "POWER".

Some believers have said; there was never a commandment to receive or seek after the Baptism with the Holy Ghost. And that you do not find the receiving of the Holy Ghost after Acts chapter nineteen. That is true.

The reason being is that receiving the Baptism with the Holy Ghost after the Day of Pentecost was the norm.

The pattern was, if the believers did not receive at the time of the new birth, someone ministered the Holy Spirit unto them shortly there after. On the other side of the coin, you cannot dedicate the whole book to this subject; there are other things to talk about. By the time we see the Apostle Paul ministering in Ephesus in Acts nineteen, the pattern of receiving the Baptism with the Holy Ghost and the operation and manifestation of the Spiritual Gifts was well established.

Now, let us turn our attention to the Day of Pentecost. The message on the Day of Pentecost uttered by the Apostle Peter included a profound statement.

Acts 2:36-39

[38]Then Peter said unto them, Repent, and he baptized every one of you in the name of Jesus Christ for the remission of sins, and ye shall receive the gift of the Holy Ghost. [39]**For the promise is unto you, and to your children, and to all that are afar off, even as many as the Lord our God shall call.**

The promise of the Father, received by Jesus, was given to the whole body of Christ. Not just to the Apostles; as some teach and believe. The Holy Spirit that fell on the Day of Pentecost was received by all 120 [The 120 represented the whole body of Christ at that time] in the upper room. This outpouring included the Apostles, men, and women. This Baptism with the Holy Ghost is available unto every born again believer. However, it is up to him or her to receive this precious gift of the Holy Ghost. If this Baptism with the Holy Spirit is not for us to day, why is it that millions of born again believers have received this "POWER" after being saved for years? If the Gifts of the

Holy Spirit are not for us today, why do we have millions of born again believers in Christ anointed and operating in the Gifts today?

The truth of the matter is that *you* are not going to receive this Baptism with the Holy Ghost if: (1) you got your mind made up that it is not for believers in Christ today. (2) You believe and were taught that it was only for the Apostles to get the church started. (3) You believe that the Baptism with the Holy Spirit, the Gifts of the Holy Spirit, and the anointing of God was done away with now that we have the Bible.

My friend, on the contrary, if you are born again and are earnestly seeking for the anointing of God with a singleness of heart, mind, and purpose; then let me tell you how to obtain it.

First, I want to tell you to make sure that you are saved-born again. If you are already born again, its ok, make your confession in Jesus Christ again. Say it out loud! I make my confession all the time. Sometime while riding along in my truck or car ministering unto the Lord.

This is the way I make my confession: *"Father in the name of Jesus, I believe in my heart and confess with my mouth that Jesus is the Messiah, the Son of the true and living God. I believe that Jesus is the Savior, who died on the cross for the sin of the world and mine. Therefore, I ask in the name of Jesus that you forgive me for all of my sins, willful and secret sins. I also believe in the death, burial, and resurrection of Jesus Christ according to the Holy Scriptures. Not only do I believe on Jesus in my heart and confess Him with my mouth, I also receive Him as my Lord, my Savior, and mighty God. Thank you Father in the Name of Jesus Christ for my salvation amen."*

This prayer will confirm your faith in Jesus Christ and put the devil on the run. The enemy will not stay around you much when you *maintain* your confession of faith.

Read the salvation scriptures again. The salvation scriptures will help you reconfirm your faith.

Scriptures like:

John 3:16

¹⁶*For God so loved the world, that he gave his only begotten Son, that whosoever believeth in him should not perish, but have everlasting life.*

John 5:24

²⁴*Verily, verily, I say unto you, He that heareth my word, and believeth on him that sent me, hath everlasting life, and shall not come into condemnation; but is passed from death unto life.*

John 3:3

³*Jesus answered and said unto him, Verily, verily, I say unto thee, Except a man be born again, he cannot see the kingdom of God.*

Ephesians 2; 8-9

⁸*For by grace are ye saved through faith; and that not of yourselves: it is the gift of God:* ⁹*Not of works, lest any man should boast.*

Second, search your heart. See to it that you do not have hidden sins in your life or anything against your brother. If so, confess your sins out loud unto the Lord. Confess those sins you have committed by name unto Him. Go also and make things right with your brother or sister. This will line your heart and spirit up to receive from the Lord.

Acts 2:38

[38]Then Peter said unto them, Repent, and be baptized every one of you in the name of Jesus Christ for the remission of sins, and ye shall receive the gift of the Holy Ghost.

Good! Now that you have made you confession of faith in Jesus Christ and repented of all sins, and you are saved, you are ready to be baptized with the Holy Ghost.

Again I say unto you, if you have believed, confessed, repented, and received Jesus Christ as your Lord and savior you are ready to receive POWER! (Some receive the new birth and the baptism with the Holy Ghost at the same time).

The word of God cites several conditions by which the Holy Spirit is given. (a) We must accept by faith Jesus Chris as Lord and Savior and turn from sin and the world. (b) Turn from the things that offend God and become "a vessel of honor, sanctified, and meet for the master's use" (2 Timothy 2:21). (c) We must desire to be filled. One should have a deep hunger and thirst to be baptized with the Holy Ghost. (John 7:37-39; Isaiah 44:3; Matthew 5:6; 6:33). (d) Prayer is always in order. We often receive the Holy Spirit in answer to definite pray (Luke 11:13; Acts 1:14; 2:1-4; 4:31; 8:15, 17). (e) We should expect Jesus to keep His promise and baptize us with the Holy Ghost (Mark 11:24; Acts 1:4-5)

Mark 11:24

Therefore I say unto you, What things soever ye desire, when ye pray, believe that ye receive *them*, and ye shall lave *them*.

Acts 1:4-5

And, being assembled together with *them*, commanded them that they should not depart from Jerusalem, but wait for the promise of the Father, which, *saith he*, ye have heard of me. ⁵For John truly baptized with water; but ye shall be baptized with the Holy Ghost not many days hence.

Third, let us take a look at Jesus. Christ Himself did not enter into His ministry until He had been "anointed... with he Holy Ghost and with power..." (See Acts 10:38)

Acts 10:38

˙ˢHow God anointed Jesus of Nazareth with the Holy Ghost and with power: who went about doing good, and healing all that were oppressed of the devil; for God was with him.

Luke 4:1

And Jesus being full of the Holy Ghost returned from Jordan, and was led by the Spirit into the wilderness.

Luke 4:18-19

The Spirit of the Lord *is* upon me, because he hath anointed me to preach the gospel to the poor; he hath sent me to heal the brokenhearted, to preach deliverance to the captives, and recovering of sight to the blind, to set at liberty them that are bruised, ¹⁹To preach the acceptable year of the Lord.

Jesus is our example. Every thing Jesus did – His preaching, His healing, his suffering, His victory over sin - He did by the power of the Holy Spirit. If Jesus could do nothing apart from the working of the Holy Ghost, how much more do we need the Spirit's anointing of power, to work the works of Christ? (Luke 4:1, 14, 18; John 3:34; Acts 1:2; 10:38).

He was baptized with the Holy Ghost and with power. The Spirit came upon Jesus to equip Him with power for His work of redemption (Luke 3: 22). Jesus Himself would later baptize His followers in the Holy Spirit so that they too might have the anointing of power (Matthew 3:11; Acts 1:5,8; 2:4).

A believer can be regenerated and indwell by the Holy Spirit, but still not be baptized with the Holy Ghost. What we must realize is that the Baptism with the Holy Spirit is an operation distinct and separate from His regeneration work.

Let's clear the air on one thing. First, we should understand that not everyone receives the Baptism with the Holy Ghost the same way. You may be in the same church meeting; you may have an instant experience, someone may lay hands on you to receive, or anoint you with oil. You may receive at home, riding along in your automobile, during your private devotion unto the Lord or while someone privately minister the Holy Spirit unto you. In other words, there is no set pattern.

Through the years people have incorporated so many man made traditions; we don't know what to follow. I admit some church groups may follow one pattern more than another but; it doesn't mean that you have to do it exactly as they do. The key to it all is that the *Holy Spirit baptizes us according to His will and not according to how we ministers unto them.*

Fourth, If someone is ministering the Holy Spirit unto you by the laying on of hands (this is one way a believer may receive), you should expect to speak in tongues when the power of God come upon you. Remember the one laying on of hands cannot give you the Holy Ghost. His prayers, intercession, and act of faith can bring God's power on people, but they must *receive on* their own.

The Holy Spirit will supernaturally give you the utterances to speak but you (man, woman or child. Yes even children 8, 9, 10, 11, and 12 years old receive the Baptism with the Holy Ghost and speak in tongues.) do the speaking. He will give you supernatural words, the power and ability in your spirit, upon your lips, and tongue, but you must do the speaking. When the Holy Spirit *fall* upon you, release yourself unto Him and let Jim *fill* you with His power.

The key is that the Holy Spirit gives the utterances, but man does the speaking.

Acts 2:4

And THEY were all filled with the Holy Ghost, and BEGAN, TO SPEAK with other tongues, as the SPIRIT GAVE THEM UTTERANCE.

Look carefully at the highlighted cap words in the text above. "They" is the subject of the sentence. *They* (the hundred and twenty) did the speaking. The Holy Ghost gave *them* the utterance.

You could say, "When THEY were filled with the Holy Ghost THEY BEGAN TO SPEAK with other tongues AS THE SPIRIT GAVE THEM UTTERANCE."

There is one point I want you to share with you my brother or sister in Christ. If you are in a church meeting with Spirit filled believers, at home, or where ever and you are being ministered to, to receive the Baptism with the Holy Spirit; those spirit fill brothers or sisters will know when the Holy Spirit is moving upon you.

Let me a sure you that most of the saints who assist in helping believers receive the Baptism with the Holy Spirit have years of experience. They have years of experience in he operation, manifestation, and Gifts of the Holy Spirit. In other words, they know what they are doing (in the power of the Spirit) and are not easily fooled by a counterfeit.

Acts 10:44-46

⁴While Peter yet spake these words, the Holy Ghost fell on all them which heard the word. ⁴⁵And they of the circumcision which believed were astonished, as many as came with Peter, because that on the Gentiles also was poured out the gift of the Holy Ghost. ⁴⁶For THEY IEARD THEM SPEAK WITH TONGUES, and magnify sod.

Acts 19:6

⁶And when Paul had laid *his* hands upon them, the Holy Ghost came on them; and THEY SPAKE WITH TONGUES, and prophesied.

Another point to remember is that tongues (gift) and prophecy (gift) are usually associated with receiving the Baptism with the Holy Ghost. Tongues are the initial sign. However, both the *gift of tongues* and *gift of prophecy* are list as one of the nine gifts of the Holy Spirit (1 Corinthians 12).

1 Cor. 14:18

18 I thank my God; **I speak with tongues** more than ye all:

1 Cor. 14:2

[2]For **he that speaketh in an *unknown* tongue** speaketh not unto men, but unto God: for no man understandeth *him;* howbeit in the spirit he speaketh mysteries.

1Cor. 14:27

[27]**If any man speak** in an *unknown* tongue, *let it be* by two, or at the most *by* three, and *that* by course; and let one interpret.

Paul said in First Corinthians 14, *"I thank my God, I* ***speak with tongues*** *more than ye all" (v.* 18); ***"He that speaketh*** ***in an unknown tongue*** *speaketh not unto men, but unto God: for no man understandeth him; howbeit in the spirit he speaketh mysteies" (v.* 2); ***"If any man speak*** *in an unknown tongue..."* *(v27).*

Acts 19:6 says, *"And when Paul had laid his hands upon them, the Holy Ghost came on them; and* ***they spake with*** ***tongues*** *and* ***prophesied.***"

Therefore, believers can expect to speak with other tongues when they are baptized with the Holy Spirit, as the Spirit gives them the utterance.

I believe that when a believer is baptized with the Holy Spirit he or she receives one or more of the gifts of the Holy Spirit listed in 1 Corinthians 12. At the same time the Holy Spirit will *enhance* and *enable* any natural talent that one may have by the *power of* the Holy Spirit.

In the next chapter I want to share with you how to receive *Power for Service* through the Baptism with the Holy Ghost.

Chapter 7

Seven Steps to Holy Ghost Power

Let me speak more to the point. Do you seriously want to receive power, the baptism with the Holy Ghost? If *your* answer is yes, then there are seven things (**Note: the Bible does not teach seven things for you to do. But, there are <u>seven</u> things that you can do**), to line *your faith, confession and your spirit up with the word of God* that you may receive the Baptism with the Holy Ghost," **The Promise of POWER.**" The key here is that when we don't know about a certain Bible subject, we need some to lead us into understanding what it takes to gain the knowledge of the subject. In other words, that we may know what it takes to get the answer.

Acts 2:38

[38]Then Peter said unto them, Repent, and be baptized ever one of you in the name of Jesus Christ for the remission o sins, and ye shall receive the gift of the Holy Ghost.

John 3:16

For God so loved the world, that he gave his only begotten Son, that whosoever believeth in him should not perish, but have everlasting life.

First step: *Believe on Jesus;* put your faith entirely of Him for what He has done for salvation and life. We are to rest absolutely on what He has already done (John 3:16-17).

Second Step: *Repentance,* even if you are already saved born again; repent of all willful and secret sins. Remember Jesus is our example; even though He was with out sin, He humble Himself to the will of the Father (Acts 2:38).

Acts 2:38

[38] *Then Peter said unto them, Repent, and be baptized even one of you in the name of Jesus Christ for the remission of sins and ye shall receive the gift of the Holy Ghost.*

Third Step: *Confession and Obedience,* Jesus humble himself and God exalted Him (Luke 3:21-22). Likewise, we nut humble ourselves to make an open confession before the Lord and the world of our renunciation of sin and our acceptance of Jesus Christ, by baptism. Our faith and hope must depend entirely upon the redemptive work of Jesus Christ. It is important to understand that the baptism with the Holy Ghost may precede water baptism. In fact, many have come forward to be saved, and received the Baptism with the Holy Spirit the same day or night they got saved. This was he case with the household of Corneluis (Acts 10:44-47).

Mat 10:32

Whosoever therefore shall confess me before men, him will I confess also before my Father which is in heaven.

Eph 2:8-9

For by grace are ye saved through , faith; and that not of yourselves: it is the gift of God: [9] Not of works, lest any man should boast.

Titus 3:5

Not by works of righteousness which we have done, but according to his mercy he saved us, by the washing of regeneration, and renewing of the Holy Ghost;

Obedience, to God's will, means a total surrender to all that He commands; to obey Him in all things. This is clearly implied in Acts 2:38, but it is brought out more explicitly in Acts 5:32 *"[32]And we are his witnesses of these things; and so is also the Holy Ghost, whom God hath given to them that obey him."*

Forth Step: *Surrender,* to the will of God. We must surrender our whole body, soul, and spirit to God. Let the Holy Spirit have His way in your life.

"He that spared not his own Son, but delivered him up for us all, how shall he not with him also freely give us all things?

Psalms 84:11

[r]For the LORD God is a sun and shield: the LORD will give grace and glory: no good thing will he withhold from them that walk uprightly.

Fifth Step: *Thirst,* we must desire to be filled. One should have a deep hunger and thirst to be baptized with the Holy Ghost. (John 7:37-39; Isaiah 44:3; Matthew 5:6; 6:33).

John 7:37-39

[37] *In the last day, that great day of the feast, Jesus stood and cried, saying, If any man thirst, let him come unto me, and drink.* [37] *He that believeth on me, as the scripture hath said, out of his belly shall flow rivers of living water.* [39] *(But this spoke he of the Spirit, which they that believe on him should receive: for the Holy Ghost was not yet given; because that Jesus was not yet glorified.)*

Sixth Step: *Prayer,* one of the most basic principles of God's word is *prayer.* Simply go to God in prayer and ask Him to baptize you with the Holy Ghost. Remember, the Holy Spirit was given to the church as a whole at Pentecost, but each individual must still appropriate the gift for himself

Luke 11:13

[13] *If ye then, being evil, know how to give good gifts unto your children: how much more shall your heavenly Father give the Holy Spirit to them that ask him?*

Seventh Step: *Faith,* again one of the basic principles of God's word is *faith.* Our duty is to simply believe God's word and act accordingly. We may not understand some things about God's word but we are to simply believe.

But let him ask in faith, nothing wavering. For he that wavereth is like a wave of the sea driven with the wind and tossed. [7] *For let not that man think that he shall receive any thing of the Lord.*

1 John 5:14

""And this is the confidence that we have in him that, if we ask any thing according to his will he heareth us:

We should expect Jesus to keep His promise and baptize us with the Holy Ghost (Mark 11:24; Acts 1:4-5).

In the next chapter I want to share with you how I received the Baptism with the Holy Ghost.

Chapter 8

How I received the Baptism with the Holy Ghost

How it all got started in our family

In 1957 the Holy Spirit began to move upon our family. The area in which we lived (Between Leesburg and Eustis Florida) was called Orange Bend, Florida across the river was known as Lisbon, Florida. The river separated the two. We lived in the country about five miles east of Leesburg. Orange Bend and Lisbon is located on Highway 44 between Leesburg and Eustis, Florida. We lived on route 2, on six acres of land.

My Father was a share cropper farmer. I've never known my Father to hold a regular job, other than farm related work of some kind. My Father loved to dig in the ground, farming and living off the land was his life.

It was twelve (12) children it our family, eight (8) girls and four (4) boys. Whew! By the grace of God, we never went hungry. There were too many things on the six acres to eat. Believe it or not, we all lived in a two Bedroom house. The house originally had two bedrooms, a kitchen, and a small living room. Later, my Father added on a third bedroom and a new kitchen to the front of the house. That made room for the boys to have their own rooms. The two younger boys: in the old kitchen (Which He turned into a bed room) area, and my older brother and I in the new bed room on the front of the house. That left the girls two beds (one large bed and one smaller bed) in the large bedroom.

My mother and father, uncle and aunt were members of the local AME Zion Methodist Church. There were also another Methodist Church, one Baptist Church, and a Church of God.

As a young boy growing up, I remember attending the Methodist, my mother and father's church, the Baptist church and the Methodist church nearest to the stores in the neighborhood. The Church of God was known as the Holiness Church. I never really attend there until after I was saved.

As we grew older, things began to change. My elder Brother was gone most of the time. Then my elder sister married a young man, his family was with the Church of God. His family was saved and filled with the Holy Ghost. That started it. My elder sister united with the Church of God and got filled with the Holy Ghost. Then my mother started visiting the Church of God to fellowship with my sister. Almost, every time my mother would attend the church of God someone would tell her about receiving the Holy Ghost. My mother said; I keep telling them that I received the Holy Ghost when I was born again, when I got saved. That didn't matter they just kept telling her that she needed the Holy Ghost.

One day, some one told her, yes, you are saved, but you don't have any power. What you need is the Baptism with the Holy Ghost. During those days they prayed; cried, groaned, rolled on the floor, and called on the name of Jesus half of the night trying to receive the Baptism with the Holy Ghost. My mother could clearly see that something was different about those saints. She could see that they had a bold testimony, joy, boldness, and power that she didn't have. So, after a period of fellowship, and observing those saints she said, well, if there be any Holy Ghost that I can receive I'm going to get it.

Not long after then, the Church of God held a revival a few riles out of town. My mother was invited to attend. She had already made up her mind that she would receive this power, this Baptism with the Holy Ghost. However, little did my mother know; this revival would change her life forever! Mother did go to the revival. I don't remember how many lights she attended. But, one thing that I do know, and that is, she came home one night Baptized with the Holy Ghost. She was speaking in other or unknown tongues as the Holy Spirit gave the utterance, shouting, praising and magnifying God. We stayed up that night until about one o'clock in the morning. The children all knew that this was the power of God upon our mother. We all took notice that night of what God was doing. Truly, the Glory of God had visited our house.

Shortly after my mother's Pentecostal experience, she began to attend the Church of God regularly. Naturally, she would take all the younger children with her. The Church of God had services twice on Sunday, Wednesday night and Friday night. Friday night was known as "POWER NIGHT." This was the time that they labored in prayer before God, and seek the Lord Jesus Christ. In addition, on Friday they would labor in prayer with any member at the Alter, who had not received the Baptism with the Holy Ghost: that they might receive. Sometimes they would fast and pray from Wednesday until Friday night.

It wasn't long before mother moved her church membership to the Church of God. Immediately following, all of my sisters and younger brothers got saved and filled with the Holy Ghost. You talking about a time singing and praising God around the house, they had a time; but I held out. Singing was in my family. First, my mother could sing, and almost all of my sisters could sing. Even I could sing.

The next turning point was; my best friend got saved and filled with the Holy Ghost. He united with the Church of God. I believed on the Lord but I had not come forward and made an open confession and united with a local church.

I use to talk with my friend about he Lord, and I notice when he and I talked about the Lord and the church, every once in a while I would feel something like a jolt of electricity in my body. So one day as we talked about the Lord it happened, so I told him about it. He said that's it; that's it! I said what? He said man that's the Holy Ghost. If you just give up, He will come in and fill you.

Well, we didn't talk much about it any more. It would just happen! The Holy Spirit would quicken me even around the house when my mother and sisters would be singing. Sometime they would see me jump when the power of God would quicken in me. One of my sisters would tease me from time to time saying, oh, that was just a mosquito that bit you. However, I believed they knew what was going on.

As time past on, with so much singing, praying, shouting, thank you Jesus, and praising God around the House, I thought that I would seek Jesus for myself. So I got in earnest, privately, every chance I got, on a daily bases. I probably was already saved but didn't know it. *But I wanted more!* **I wanted the Power and the Anointing.**

There was not a day past that I was not calling on the name of Jesus, asking Him to save me. I was calling, Jesus, Jesus, Jesus, Lord save me, Lord Come into my life. This went on for at least two months. In the mean time the Baptist church had a revival. I remember being outside the church one night during the revival with one or two of the young men my age. Church service had already started. The last young man said to me, you better come on in, everybody else is joining. I said no; I'm not going in. Immediately, he went inside leaving me outside alone.

Little did he know; the Spirit of the Lord was upon me that night. Something would not let me go in that church that night. I thought about what I said to the Lord one day when I was about twelve, cutting wood for the house. While cutting wood and meditating on the Lord one day, I stop cutting, and stood the axe up, looked up toward heaven and said, Lord, if I ever be anything in life: I want to be it for you. Then I recalled what the preacher would say when he ask some one to be saved. He would walk up and down the front rows with his hand stretched out saying, "give me your hand and God your heart." But, I still couldn't go inside. I said to my self; Lord, there has to be more. It had to be, because I could feel Him working in my spirit. So that night, I headed for home.

I believe the Holy Spirit began to really do a work in us, our family, between the month of May and August of 1957. It was during the summer when school was out that my friend got saved, and I really started seeking the Lord. We had summer jobs working in the citrus nursery and orange groves. But that didn't stop me from praying and seeking the Lord morning and evening.

The truck that came to pick up the workers would always past my house and go about a half a mile down the road to pickup other workers. I would always catch the truck on the return trip.

One morning, while waiting to catch the truck on the return trip, I started to really pray and seek the Lord. All of a sudden, while standing on the side of the road, I was shaken by the power of the Holy Ghost. At first, I thought it would be just like any other time that I had felt the Holy Spirit. No! This wasn't the case. The Holy Ghost jolted me and came upon my whole body.

My body was buzzing and tingling as if you had 220 volts of electricity connected to me. I realized that I could not move any thing but my eyes. It was as if I was glued to the road with a power upon me that I had never experienced before.

Then suddenly, a ball of light or fire about the size of a basketball appeared in the road in front of me about 20-30 feet away. Immediately this ball of light or fire I cannot tell: burst in to a brilliant soft white light. This light covered everything. I could not see through the light or anything beyond the light. It was as if the road went up to the light and stopped.

To my amazement, Jesus appeared standing in the mist of the light with a white robe on all the way down covering His feet. The light looked as if it was radiating out from Jesus. No light was shining toward me, but the light from Him was radiating outward and upward.

Jesus started walking toward me. When He got about half way to me, a movement downward caught my attention. I notice that as He step His knee would push the robe out and His feet would come out from under the robe. He appeared to have some type of sandals on his feet. To my amazement: Jesus feet; did not appear to be touching the ground. It was as if, He was walking about 3 inches above the ground.

The next thing I knew, Jesus was about 5-7 feet in front of me. He stopped. We were looking face to face. I was still buzzing, radiating, and locked down with the Holy Ghost. Slowly He started raising His arms upward. As I looked at His arms, the big sleeves of the robe hang down from His arms. When He stop raising His arms, as we looked at each other, I heard His say, "COME!" But I never saw His mouth move. Immediately it was as if someone turned the power of the Holy Spirit up a few notches on me, and I momentarily lost consciousness. Swoosh, Jesus was gone and I was back to the natural.

After coming back to the natural, I looked down the road about 150 yards away; the truck was coming. The first thing that I thought was that the people on the truck had just witness what had happen to me. Then I began to think; was I shouting, dancing under the Holy Spirit or what? A few seconds latter the truck arrived. The three people in the cab said good morning, those on the back of the truck said good morning, amazingly, they never saw a thing. They didn't say a thing about it, so I didn't say anything.

This took place on Thursday or Friday; the third week in August 1957. The next week, the last week of August, the AME Zion Methodist Church, had a revival. I attended that revival. But the most amazing thing happened to me. From those days to this day I cannot remember Monday through Thursday of that week of the revival.

The only thing that I can remember is that I was at the revival that Thursday night. I can't remember how I got there. I cannot remember going in the church that night. I cannot remember any of the revival service that night. When I came to my self that night, I was in the church; we were all standing for dismissal. I remember being on the right side of the church, third pew from the front row. The preacher was dismissing for the night. I continued to stand and watch the people clear the 1St, 2nd, 3rd, and 4th set of pews; but I didn't move.

Then suddenly, a movement caught my attention at the end of my pew in the aisle. It was Deacon Robinson. He was looking at me, and then he hailed the people. Hey, the Spirit of the Lord is upon this young man he exclaimed, I can feel It. Everyone come back inside! They came back inside; ask me to get on my knees at the Alter. They began to sing a hymn and my best friend's mother, sister Wright, got down beside me and began to pray. I thought to my self, well I haven't felt that quickening power tonight.

By this time the church had really picked up the hymn, and Sister Wright and others really began to pray in earnest. So I said to my self, well I'll just put my mind on Jesus and seek Him like I do when I'm by myself. Then I shut everything else out and locked in on seeking Jesus, the first thing happen was that power that came on me when Jesus appeared to me on the side of the road, came just around my mouth, then in my mouth but no where else on my body. My mouth started slowly opening until it was wide open.

The power of the Holy Ghost was radiating, buzzing, and tingling all around and in my mouth. I tried gently twice to close my mouth buy I couldn't. When I realized that I couldn't close my mouth, I gave way to the

Holy Spirit that was upon me. Instantly when I gave way to the Holy Spirit my whole body was quicken by the Spirit and I momentarily lost consciousness. When I came back to the natural for a few moments, I realized that I was up shouting, and speaking it unknown tongues as hard as I could go. I could see that about three of the saints (Ladies) had join hands and form a circle around me.

Suddenly I felt something hanging from my arms as I was shouting. I remember looking but I could not see anything. Then immediately, it was revealed to me what it was. It was tags of fire or flames of fire that I could actually feel as my arms swing through the air as I was shouting but I could not see it. That was the last thing I remembered at the church. I went out under the Holy Spirit.

When I came to myself, I was home about two miles from the church, sitting in the living room in a straight back chair. My mother had her hand on my shoulder steadying me in the chair. I was still speaking in unknown tongues and the Holy Spirit jolting me.

It wasn't long before I calm down a little more, and my mother realized that I had my consciousness back. The first thing that I heard her say was, "Son, the Lord really got hold of you tonight." A few moments later I heard her say, "We are having tarrying service tomorrow night (Friday night), why don't you come and go with us?" I said, ok! I didn't know much about the tarrying service at the Church of God, but I went. That Friday night at the tarrying service, I was astounded. The saints there as far as I could tell were baptized with the Holy Ghost. They had some of that same anointing that I had just received. The saints at the Church of God were unlike the saints of other churches that I had attended. These saints had a boldness, praise and worship was or their lips, a powerful testimony and an anointing of the Holy Spirit that I had no seen among the saint of other churches. Shortly after, I united with the Church of God and was baptized.

Immediately following, I started to have visions at night. Night after night I would get caught up in the Spirit and my bedroom ceiling would look like a Drive Inn Theater. This went on for several years. It would even happen in the day sometime.

Then I started to receive Revelation knowledge. The Lord would reveal things to me that I could not possible know. As I grew in the Lord and became stronger in the faith and knowledge of Him, He called me to preach His word. The next thing I knew the Lord was using me in the Five-Fold Ministry and the Gifts of the Holy Spirit.

Oh how wonderful and marvelous is the mighty works of God! I thank my Lord and Savior Jesus Christ for Salvation and life, and the wonderful Baptism with the Holy Ghost. I pray that you to will receive this wonderful *"Promise of the Father."* Let Jesus baptize you with the Holy Ghost for *power and service.*

Chapter 9

Recap: What we have learned

Chapter 1, what we learned:

1. The prophet Joel prophesied about the outpouring of the Holy Spirit upon all flesh.

2. John the Baptist received a revelation from God that there would be One who would baptize with the Holy Ghost.

3. Jesus said that believers would be baptized with the Holy Ghost.

4. The Holy Spirit came on His divine mission on the Day of Pentecost.

5. The Holy Spirit is the "Promise of the Father."

6. Believers can be baptized with the Holy Spirit and speak in tongues as the Spirit give them the utterance.

7. Three baptisms are available for all born again believers. (1) Baptism into the Body of Christ. (2) Baptism in water, and (3) the Baptism with the Holy Spirit. 8. What God gave to the church for the perfecting of the saints and the unity of the Body of Christ!

9. Who the Holy Spirit uses in ministering to the Body of Christ.

10. The importance of the believer to say the same thing that God says according to His WORD.

11. The power and the ability of God's WORD.

12. Tongue speaking (gift) and prophecy (gift) are initial signs associated with of the Baptism with the Holy Ghost.

13. Some doctrines of men are not the Word of God.

14. There is a difference in tongues spoken on the Day of Pentecost (Other tongues) and tongues spoken in First Corinthians 14th chapter. (Unknown tongues)

15. How believers are able to speak in tongues.

16. The Baptism with the Holy Spirit is available unto every born again believer.

17. In the Old Testament only three types of people had the Holy Spirit, the King, Priest, and the Prophet.

Chapter 2, what we learned:

1. There are two distinct operations of the Holy Spirit in regard to the New Birth and the Baptism with the Holy Ghost.

2. The regeneration work of the Holy Spirit for Salvation, is not the same work of the Spirit, for the Baptism with the Holy Spirit.

3. The Baptism with the Holy Spirit is for power and service, the regeneration; new birth is for eternal life.

4. A comparison of the scriptures on the new birth and that of the Baptism with the Holy Spirit shows clearly that they are not for the same purpose.

5. The New Birth and the Baptism with the Holy Spirit may take place at the same time, but both are two distinct works of the Holy Spirit each for a different purpose.

6. The Holy Spirit came on His divine mission on the Day of Pentecost.

7. The 120 followers of Christ all received the Baptism with the Holy Spirit, but they did not all received the same language. The Holy Spirit divided the language among the 120 followers of Christ.

8. The Holy Spirit imparted several (different tongues), as He will unto the 120 believers in the upper room.

9. First came the anointing, the filling, then the ability to perform.

10. When Philip preached Christ and the Kingdom of God unto the Samaritans the Lord confirmed his ministry with miracles following.

11. The Samaritans believed Philip's ministry and were baptized.

12. The Samaritans were already born again baptized believers when Peter and John arrived in Samaria.

13. After Peter and John arrived in Samaria they called a meeting with the new converts, and prayed for them that they might receive the Holy Ghost.

14. Laying on of hands are not the only way one may receive the Baptism with the Holy Ghost.

15. One may receive the Baptism with the Holy Ghost different from another even in the same place at the same time.

Chapter 3, what we learned:

1. Saul of Tarsus had an encounter with Jesus on Damascus road.

2. When Saul encountered Jesus on Damascus road, he said what must I do?

3. The Lord Jesus instructed Saul to continue on into Damascus and it would be told him what he must do.

4. The Lord reveals to Ananias that Saul was a chosen vessel unto Him. Jesus also commissioned Ananias to minister unto Saul that he might receive his sight and be filled with the Holy Ghost.

5. Saul believed Ananias report, were saved, received his sight, were baptized in water, Baptized with the Holy Ghost, ate food to regain his strength, continued certain days with the disciples which were at Damascus, and straightway preached Christ that He is the Son of God.

6. When Peter preached the word at Cornelius house the Holy Ghost fell on all of them, they were all baptized with the Holy Ghost.

7. The Gentiles received the Baptism with the Holy Spirit.

8. Those of the circumcision was convinced because they heart them speak in tongues and magnify God.

Chapter 4, what we learned:

1. Paul encountered twelve disciple of John the Baptist in Ephesus. He said, have you received the Holy Ghost since you believed?

2. When they said no, we have not heard whether be any Holy Ghost, he then question about their baptism.

3. After finding a starting point to minister unto them, Paul started with the baptism and ministry of John and finished with belief in Jesus Christ.

4. The Disciples of John believed Paul's report and were baptized.

5. Paul baptized the twelve disciples then laid his hands on them that They might receive the Holy Ghost.

6. They were baptized with the Holy Ghost and spoke in tongues and prophesied.

The terms listed below all refer to the same experience

7. (A) Acts 2:4 "And they were all FILLED with the Holy Ghost."

    (B) Acts 8:17 "And they RECEIVED the Holy Ghost."

    (C) Acts 9:17 "And Be FILLED with the Holy Ghost."

    (D) Acts 10:44 "The Holy Ghost FELL on all them which heard the word."

    (E) Acts 19:1-7 "The Holy Ghost CAME on them."

It is the *Promise of the Father* to all that would believe.

Chapter 10

Prayer to receive the Baptism With the Holy Ghost

Prayer for Salvation

"Father in the name of Jesus, I believe in my heart and confess with my mouth that Jesus is the Messiah the Son of the true and living God. I believe that Jesus is the Savior, who died on the cross for the sin of the world and mine. Therefore, I ask in the name of Jesus that you forgive me for all of my sins, willful and secret sins. I also believe in the death, burial, and resurrection of Jesus Christ according to your Word. Not only do I believe on Jesus in my heart and confess Him with my mouth, I also receive Him as my Lord, my Savior and mighty God. Bless me now Lord, that I may worship you in spirit and truth. I surrender my all unto you. Take me and use me Lord in thy service, according to thy own will and purpose. Thank you Father, in the Name of Jesus Christ for my salvation amen."

Prayer to receive the Baptism with the Holy Ghost

Most Holy and everlasting Father in the name of Jesus Christ my Lord and savior, I pray thee master that thou would hear my plea.

I pray thee that thou would cleanse me, and purge me of all sins and unrighteousness.

Bless me now Lord, that I may worship you in spirit and truth. I surrender my all unto you. Take me and use me Lord in thy service, according to thy own will and purpose.

Lord, I believe the Holy Scriptures concerning the receiving, filling, and baptism with the Holy Ghost. Master, it is written in the Holy Scriptures with promise to those who believe on the Lord Jesus. Therefore Lord, I desire with all my heart, praying, and *asking thee that I receive the promise of the Father. Fill me Lord with this Gift, for it is promised unto all thy people.*

Lord I desire to receive the Baptism with the Holy Ghost with all my heart. I desire to receive even as the Samaritans did who believed and was baptized at the preaching of Philip and the laying on of hands of Peter and John.

I pray the Lord that I may be Baptized with the Holy Ghost even as the Gentiles received at Cornelius house at the preaching of Peter. I pray to receive even as the twelve disciples of John the Baptist who received the Baptism with the Holy Ghost at the preaching of Paul in Ephesus. Lord the scriptures says that they spoke in tongue, glorifying thee, magnifying thee and prophesying in thy name.

Even so Lord, I desire to receive, for it is written in the scriptures... "If any man thirst, let him come unto me, and drink." Lord it is also written... "If ye then, being evil, know how to give good gifts unto your children; how much more shall your heavenly Father give the Holy Spirit to them that ask Him?"

I pray the Lord Jesus for this Blessed Gift. In thy name I now expect to receive the Baptism with the Holy Ghost with boldness and power. Impart unto me Spiritual Gifts, that I may work the works of Jesus Christ. In the name of Jesus manifest thy glory in me, and use me in thy service. Amen,

This is how most of the saints at the Church where I were Pastor received the Baptism with the Holy Ghost. They received by praying this prayer.

This is the prayer that the Lord inspired me to write, and was given to the saints at the Oak Grove Missionary Baptist Church (those who wanted to receive the Baptism with the Holy Ghost).

I would give them this prayer on Sunday and instruct them to go home and pray this prayer for the week. The next Sunday, I would ask if they were ready to receive. Their answer would always be YES! At the end of the service, I would take them (only the group who had prayed for the week) off to the side, into the choir room.

Then I would read to them two different scriptures from the Bible (where believers received the Baptism with the Holy Ghost in the Bible). I would then explain unto them what they should expect the Lord to do for them.

Next, I would pray for them to receive the Baptism with the Holy Ghost and instantly, they had a Pentecostal experience. The power of God would fall upon each of them. They were baptized with the Holy Ghost! They received instantly, the Promise of the Father every time.

This is the way the Lord led me to minister the Holy Ghost unto them (This was a group receiving all at one time). However, this is not the only way they received. Even the children, some at 8,10, 11, and 12 years of age at our church received the Baptism with Holy Ghost and spoke in tongues. If they can receive the baptism of the Holy Ghost; what about you?

Remember: JESUS promised power to the believers and followers of Christ.

John 1:33

[33]*And I knew him not: but he that sent me to baptize with water, the same said unto me, Upon whom thou shalt see the Spirit descending, and remaining on him, the same is he which baptizeth with the Holy Ghost.*

Luke 3:16

[16]*John answered, saying unto them all, I indeed baptize you with water; but one mightier than I cometh, the latchet of whose shoes I am not worthy to unloose: he shall baptize you with the Holy Ghost and with fire:*

John 14:14-17

[14]If ye shall ask any thing in my name, I will do it. [15]If ye love me, keep my commandments. [16]And I will pray the Father, and he shall give you another Comforter, that he may abide with you for ever; [17]Even the Spirit of truth; whom the world cannot receive, because it seeth him not, *neither knoweth him: but ye know him; for he dwelleth with you, and shall be in you.*

Acts 1:4-5

[4]*And, being assembled together with them, commanded then that they should not depart from Jerusalem, **but wait for the promise of the Father,** which, saith he, ye have heard of me For John truly baptized with water; but **ye shall be baptizer with the Holy Ghost not many days hence.***

Acts 1:8

But ye shall receive power, after that the Holy Ghost is come upon you: *and ye shall be witnesses unto me both if Jerusalem, and in all Judaea, and in Samaria, and unto the uttermost part of the earth.*

Acts 2:38-39

*Then Peter said unto them, Repent, and be baptized every one of you in the name of Jesus Christ, for the remission of sins **and ye shall receive the gift of the Holy Ghost.*** [39] **For the promise is unto you, and to your children, and to all that an afar off, even as many as the Lord our God shall call.**

Notes

Notes

Notes

Notes

Ovit G. Pursley Ministries®
Sow a Seed Today

*...Pay thy vows unto the most high and
call upon me in the day of trouble;
I will deliver thee...Psalm: 50:14-15*

Jesus is coming soon!

This is a good work, anointed of the Lord Jesus Christ.

Note: All Glory, Honor, Praise, and Thanksgiving is given unto God the Father, the Lord Jesus Christ, and the Holy Spirit for the wisdom and knowledge to compile all books by *Ovit G. Pursley Ministries.*

Ovit G. Pursley Ministries Publishes Books, Bible studies for the Christian Market. The mission is to save, teach, strengthen, and establish believers in the faith. To provide a way for Ministers and Lay people to know Christ and make -Him known by publishing life-related materials that are Biblically rooted and: culturally reverent.

Ovit G. Pursley Personal Commission: "Go save, confirm, strengthen and establish believers in the Faith. Ministering both to the Spiritual and Physical needs of God's people, especially those who are starving for the sincere milk and meat of the Word. And lo I am with you always."

NOTICE: To Pastors, Ministers, Church Groups or Bible Study Groups; you may order in bulk (Large number of books for your congregation or study group). When doing so we recommend that you collect all money for each book and write a (one) check from the church or study group for the order. Thank You. Make an Order Today!

Do something before it's too late!!!
Help me bless the body of Christ!
Sow a Seed Today!

Note: All Gifts, Love Offering, Contributions, and Seed Sowing into this Ministry are nightly appreciated to support this great work of God for the body of Christ.

❑ I believe this is a work anointed of God! My Seed-Gift is:

❑ $50 ❑ $100 ❑ $200 ❑ $500 ❑ $1,000 ❑ $_____

❑   Enclosed is $_____ toward *my* Vow of Faith.

Please make all checks and money orders payable (in U.S. FUNDS ONLY) to *Ovit G. Pursley Ministries* and send order with remittance to:

Ovit G. Pursley Ministries
11130 Kingston Pike, Ste. 103
Knoxville, Tennessee 37934

"Give, and it shall be given unto you; good measure, pressed down, and shaken together, and running over, shall men give into your bosom. For with the same measure that ye mete withal it shall be measured to you again."Luke 6:38

Those wishing to contact Elder Ovit Pursley personally for *Special Prayer, Contributions or to Sow Seed into this Ministry* may write in care of the following address:

Ovit G. Pursley Ministries
11130 Kingston Pike, Ste. 103
Knoxville, TN 37934

*Feel free to copy this page to send with your seed offering!
Name: _____
Address: _____
City: _____ State_____ Zip: _____
Email: _____
Phone: (   ) _____ Cell: (   ) _____

Ovit & Patricia Pursley, Sr.

About The Author

Ovit G. Pursley Sr. is a chosen vessel, called, and ordained of God to preach and teach the Gospel of Jesus Christ, and to minister to the spiritual and physical needs of His people.

He is anointed in the Five-Fold Ministry (Apostle, Pastor, Teacher, Prophet, and Evangelist); Healing, and Deliverance. He is a "Powerful Word Preacher, Teacher, and Evangelist," who proclaims; that the Power of God unto Salvation is in the "Word" the "Holy Spirit," the "Name and Blood of Jesus and the Resurrection of Jesus Christ."

He served as the senior Pastor of the Oak Grove Missionary Baptist Church of Niota, Tennessee for 14 years. He also served one (I) year as Second Vice Moderator and seven (7) years as First Vice Moderator of the Loudon District Baptist Missionary and Education Association. He also served ten (10) years as a National Evangelist. Presently: fulfilling his mission as a writer of the living word.